# The Me:
# Briages

## A memoir

*To Joy,*
*with thanks -*
*love Robbie.*

*Roberta J. Dewa*

# ROBERTA J DEWA

Glass Tortoise

*The Memory of Bridges*

Published by Glass Tortoise

© Roberta J Dewa 2013
(www.robertadewa.co.uk)

ISBN 978-0-9576119-0-0

Printed by Russell Press,
Russell House,
Bulwell Lane,
Basford,
Nottingham
NG6 0BT

# *Contents*

*For my mother*

## *Prologue*

## *The Bridge, The Book*

I am back in Wilford, standing at the Toll Bridge. It's past eleven, and I have just got off the last trolleybus of the night, walked straight across the roundabout from the terminus, leaving a trail of dark footprints in the silvery grass. The lights on the bridge lead into darkness. I pass the toll booth, its windows grilled and padlocked for the night, and start up the cobbled slope to the bridge, past the sign that says NO VEHICLES, to walk over into Wilford on the southern side of the river. The concrete slabs that make up the spans are shakier than they used to be, they shudder as I step onto them, the shudder makes its way up my legs. Through the latticework of iron supports at the sides of the bridge I get glimpses of the river, dark as ink, rushing past beneath me. It's deep, dense, preoccupied with the flood it's carrying.

As I reach the other side I look ahead. I should be able to see the lights of the Ferry Inn by now, but the lights are out, or perhaps the fog is too thick. The empty road dips down toward the village, streetlamps flushing it orange, rusty railings fencing off the fields on either side. I can smell the fog and the wet grass and the rusty metal, I can hear the lapping of disturbed water from the Ballast Hole, its torpedo basin out of sight in the darkness. Nothing else is moving. The ponies have been taken away, or they are settled down for the night somewhere I can't see.

I start to run. Something is happening at home, something I must get back in order to prevent. The fog swells on my forehead, weighs it down. I turn left into Coronation Avenue, pass the Catholic school on my right. The field is on my left side now, the line of sycamores snowing leaves, the top bars of the railings sagging where we used to sit on them. Just before the railway arch I turn right into Vernon, run down the length of the avenue. A coloured pillar of light shines from the leaded glass panel of our front door. I reach the house, knock, and the door swings back against its frame.

I stand in the hall with my hand on the banister. I call out that I'm home.

Nobody answers.

I run up the stairs and into my bedroom. The pink nightlight gleams in the corner, softens the edges of the room. The curtains are open and there's a red glow outside pushing back the darkness, so that the line of the railway bank is just visible. And I think I smell a train. I go up to the window, listening for the rumble of the goods wagons, for the rhythm of the wheels on the track. Below me I can see that the back door is open and a wedge of light let into the garden. My mother stands in its beam, a scarf knotted underneath her chin; the soft fringed scarf she wears when her neuralgia is bad. She is standing over a smoking dustbin, burning papers, tearing pages from a stack of notebooks at her feet. Dark spots of soot circle in the glow like flies.

I recognize the notebooks. They are red, with soft covers; the ones in which she is writing her history of

Wilford. I push on the window, and then I bang on it, calling out for her to stop. She turns at the sound and looks upward, but her gaze is too high, beyond the window and the house roof.

As she turns, I realize she isn't wearing her glasses. She can't see me.

I run back downstairs, into the kitchen. It is tunnel-dark, darker than it should be with the back door open and the light of the fire outside. I feel all round the walls but I can't find the door, not the knob, the frame, anything. I go round and round, round and round, but I can't feel anything but plaster. Cold plaster, like the walls of a house that's been cold and empty for years. I can't get out to her.

When I wake up I'm still calling. Out of bed, hands on cold windows. Miles away, years away from the house in the dream.

It's only a dream, my husband says. But dreams are like fictions. The truth is hiding inside them somewhere.

It is still dark, but I can't go back to bed. I feel for a dressing gown and go out onto the landing, shutting the bedroom door quietly behind me. I sit down on the top stair and hug my knees, watching as my breath smokes upward in the chilly air. I am shivering.

But a memory is forming in the air, a memory from thirty years ago, not long before my mother died. I am in a library, the kind of library you could still find in those days, a place of silence where the sun spilled in through high windows and the dust-beams were full of words.

My mother and I sit working in this silence, on opposite sides of an oak table. We are both writing in our notebooks: my mother is working on her history of Wilford Village, and I am engaged in research for my first novel, an impassioned defence of bad King John. Although we work at the same table, we do not talk, we do not compare notes. There is an empty space on the table between us, a kind of no man's land where neither of us places our books and papers. Perhaps it is because our ideas of history are so different: my mother's chosen subject is the familiar, the village of both our childhoods, her own work a small link in a smooth continuum of history. My idea of history is that it is full of lies, lies whose truth must be exposed.

But whatever the reason, the space exists. Like the writing in which we are engaged, it is not spoken of, but it divides us as surely as a river; unoccupied, blank, unexplained.

While I am working, my mother gets up and, without a word, leaves the table. I continue writing, but slowly I become aware that she has been gone a long time. Then, just as I am about to look up, the recollection ends, or skims across the surface of a deeper memory to a time after her death.

That time is April 10th, 1983, the day after my mother's funeral. I am alone, in the spare bedroom, on hands and knees, sorting through her things. On the windowsill there are cards, mostly of condolence. *Sympathy*, they say, *In deepest sympathy*. One or two cards – the ones that say *Happy Birthday* - I have not yet taken down. In front of me on the floor, its lid propped open, is a green metal trunk, my old toybox. Spread all around me on the carpet are my mother's papers. Letters, bank statements, sketchbooks with drawings of churches and costumes for plays. Notebooks, full of drama group and village business. A commonplace book, filled with favourite poems. A folder of my childish drawings, my handmade cards to her. But there is no trace of the history of Wilford. Not a notebook, not a scrap of paper. I turn the papers over on the floor, I reach into the corners of the green box, but I hit bottom, and find nothing.

The history is not here. No book. No explanation why.

*Why.* I can hear myself whisper it. The word disperses, in a wisp of smoke. The history seems to disperse too, as if I imagined the whole thing: her writing of it, the destroying of it; as if it was no more than one of my many fictions.

I gather up the papers, replace them in the box, and shut it. I cannot deal with this, not now. Shock has closed me down. For how long the box will stay unopened, I do not know, at that time.

A bare three months later, with my husband and my father, I leave Wilford. The box comes with me, shifted into yet another spare room; and still another, when we return to Nottingham. Years pass: a decade of years, two decades. All through that time I keep my head down, writing, as if my absorption in the act of invention will prevent me from seeing that my mother is not coming back. I write stories, poems, whole novels, narratives that creep through the centuries as they move ever closer to the present day. And then – I feel it coming, as my hand seizes under me and my fingers curl back into my palm – the stories dry up and the words stop. Finally, I look up, and find myself in the present day, waking from a dream of the old life. Here, on this landing, the other side of the spare room door. The box still closed.


I get slowly to my feet. I have more a sense of absence than of loss. Something absent, that might yet be retrieved. What I see, when I look back at the moment when my mother left, is less the book she took away than the empty space between us on the table, the no man's land that we did not cross. As I think of it, with my mind empty of other stories, of lives that nobody ever lived, the story that slips into the void is that of my mother and myself, a story I seem never to have possessed, don't yet know if I can tell. But when I shut my eyes and conjure that space on the table I see words appear, words I couldn't see before. They hover in the air, waiting to be undissolved, to settle onto a new page. I can hear them in my head, but the voice I hear is my voice, not my mother's. These are not the calm words she would have written; they are stormy words, full of anger and untold secrets, full of flood and darkness and broken bridges. All the words that went missing from our lives; the truths that hid themselves in the space between us.

Finally it's morning. The light is turning from indigo to grey; a solitary treetop thrush sings into the dawn. I pull the landing curtains back halfway. Behind me, at the periphery of my vision, I see the dark oblong of the door into the spare room, resolving in the light. My dreams refuse to fade into the day. They stand their ground, waiting to give up their truth.

I put my hand on the door. I will step into the no man's land, and let the words in. But they are so many, they threaten to overwhelm me. So I start with just one word, that will take me right back, to the end of us; to the beginning.

## *1*

## *The Power House*

Wilford. The word is a soft word. No anger in it, no raised voice, no storms. It has the willows in it, the riverside willows whose branches my mother cuts each spring to watch the grey buds break open into green. And it has the river in it – ford – the river Trent before the time of Wilford's bridges, a time I do not remember, but when there was a ferryboat which served as conduit across the river until the bridge was built. A time of drownings, of limp bodies lying cold in the riverside mortuary next to St Wilfrid's Church.

But for as long as I can remember, and long before me, there are bridges, built to cross from the city to the almost-island of Wilford: a tongue of land at the southern extremity of Nottingham, formed by a meander in the River Trent; a pale blue meander thrown around the land like the loop of a skipping rope. This tongue, or isthmus, is a once-medieval village built in linear fashion along its main road, which branches out here and there into 1920s and 30s cul-de-sacs of neat brick semis, but keeps generally on a south to north course, hugging the west bank of the river as it heads for the tip of the tongue and the old Toll Bridge, the Victorian structure of brick and iron which bolts it to the world on the north side of the Trent.

To the east of the village, and bisecting the isthmus into west and eastern halves, is the almost dead-straight line of the railway embankment, carrying the goods and passengers of the Great Central Railway south to London, crossing the river by its own double bridge of massive metal piers and girder spans and dwarfing the Toll Bridge a hundred yards away. East again, and everything is green to the far shore of the isthmus: a green of fields and allotments and scrubland scrawled with the wavy lines of unofficial paths: paths to the willows along the river, paths to dens, paths to the arches of the railway viaduct, paths to the glassy water of the Ballast Hole, a lozenge of water left by a forgotten flood and stranded, like an Oxbow lake, in one of Wilford's fields. Around the fields are floodbanks, of the earthen, informal variety, that are a part of our landscape, surrounding us like Dutch dykes, good vantage-points and boundary markers. On the river side of the floodbanks nearest the bridge are fields of ponies; to the east of the isthmus, beyond the railway line, the wilderness of paths and dens and undergrowth we call the Willowwoods, a name with surely deliberate echoes of Kenneth Grahame's Wild Wood. Here, where the land is vulnerable to inundation and thus unusable, we occasionally meet with Wilford's own incarnation of stoats and weasels.

Water. Without which Wilford would have been absorbed into the city long ago, without which it would have lost its village identity, its holiday magnetism for the slum-dwellers of the Meadows, whose real meadows had long gone under terraced rows, their trees under the brick trunks of chimneys; who enjoyed the otherness of the bridge crossing, the paying of the toll, the teas served from thatched cottages and cherry-eatings in the Vicarage garden. Water, without which the village residents would not have had to move upstairs after many winters, but especially those of 1940 and 47, while the Trent forsook its loop and moved in on the village, causing engineers to visit with levels and theodolites and to raise the floodbanks higher, felling the avenue of elms along the old Bee Bank and hoisting up its horizon with earth and stone and new techniques in concrete.

Water that divides us from the industry on the north side of the river, from the spinwheel of Clifton Colliery, the power station with its Art Deco brickwork, its tall chimneys with their pink evening glow, the long aeroplane hiss of sudden escapes of steam; that protects us from the dull controlled explosions and unexplained lightning flashes emanating from the Gun Factory. These places are of Wilford, but North Wilford, caught in the photographs of early village views as blurry backdrops, hard shapes softened out by lenses fixing on the small, the near, the picturesque, the rural. Existing in a kind of willed myopia, an uncorrected defect of vision that we all have.

Lenses that we need just to go about our daily business, in the 1950s, the 1960s. So many of us are short-sighted: my grandmother, my grandfather and my mother with their bottle glasses, the sepia-brown tint to protect their eyes from sun. Turn up any photograph of the Women's Institute or the Mothers' Union and there they are, beneath the candyfloss topping of best hats; the spectacles, some black severe National Health issue, most of them winged on the top edge of the frame, blue plastic flourishes turned upward at the end like surrogate eyebrows. Without them we do not see very far, maybe to the end of the avenue, maybe as far as Mr Pearce's flame of white hair as he reads the lesson; certainly not the numbers of the hymns or the sums on the blackboard, not as far as anything that changes, that cannot be remembered. Without them we can still walk through the village in soft focus, getting our bearings from the white front of Hunter's Farm as we pass it, the green pools of the village greens, the squat Georgian huddle of the village shop, where the week's grocery order is waiting for us in a basket.

Short sight keeps us content, thankful in a postwar world where there is so much to be thankful for. The two world war generations make do and mend, they cut their loaves of bread horizontally so that the slices are holed with the tracery of lace, they save brown paper and butter wrappers and light the stove with long coloured tapers. Most of the villagers, including my own family, own no car; my family will never own one. And the Toll Bridge, its curlicues of ironwork corroding into rust-flowers beneath our feet, is already too weakened to support a bus; its weight limit falls year by year, four tons, two tons, Pedestrians Only. If there is a warning here, a sign of trouble to come, we do not heed it. We walk, as we have always done. As my grandparents did, crossing the river into Wilford for the first time, stepping from the bridge into a kind of paradise.

And for everyday needs, Wilford provides: the sweetshop with its penny box full of liquorice and glass jars of pineapple chunks and dolly mixtures; the village hall where there are dances and church socials; the pub where the beer is brought by two splendid dray-horses that leave their steaming droppings in the road, shining brown like soft horse-chestnuts; the church, breasting the bend in the river like a lighthouse, for those occasions where change feels like continuity: birth, marriage, death.

In 1922, three years before the power station comes on line, my family do not yet belong to Wilford. But they will, they qualify already by reason of their wish to belong; and curiously, also already, by reason of short sight. Both of them have it, two of the smartest people in the long queue waiting to come over the Toll Bridge on Bank Holiday Monday.

My grandparents, not long married, are waiting in the queue at the toll house to come over into Wilford, to walk around the village and take tea on the big field. Since their marriage they have lived on the north side of the river, next to the soot and smoke of the great goods yard at Queen's Walk, but their Sunday clothes are clean and well-ironed. Lillian is petite, with bright skin and dark bobbed hair; she has a weakness for hats, and her brown felt cloche is trimmed with a turquoise ribbon. Beside her my grandfather transfers his Player's Navy Cut to his mouth as he pays over the two halfpennies at the toll booth. Ted has a fierce look to him, with bristly eyebrows that slope down to the bridge of his nose, and flare out at his temples; with bottle-thick glasses that shrink his eyes to dark slits, that will one day be brown-tinted to protect what is left of his eyesight from the sun. It is a fierce look that is undeserved, a genetic legacy from the hard farming life of his Cotswold forebears, carried with dignity like the smoker's gravel in his voice.

My grandmother tucks her hand in the cool crook of his gabardined arm, and they make their way across the bridge. The river heaves grey coils of water around the cylinders driven into its bed, it curls and straightens with the current, fends off the city, lets the visitors gently down onto the slope of road running down into the village. My grandfather lifts the protective lenses from his eyes and raises his camera. The road is in the centre of the picture; the house they will buy not yet visible. The redbrick walls of the bridge fall away to green. Beyond the green, the white walls of the Ferry Inn. As they walk, Ted takes picture after picture of long low cottages still roofed with thatch, cottages named for trees, for orchards; pictures he will develop himself in the cupboard under the stairs of a brand new house, a twenties semi called, for luck, 'Rowan': a name to keep out witches, to turn trouble from those within.

And in three years, months before the power station, coaled to its gunwales, pylons handing out dark power lines north, west, and south across the city, comes on stream, there will be another picture, of my grandmother with my mother on her knee; a baby in white dress and long knitted bootees on sturdy limbs held out frog-leg fashion. A baby with a solemn face, her father's face; already with the shadow of short sight with one eye half-closed, yet somehow prescient, considering the world. This photograph, with its homeliness, is

17

nothing like the baby picture I will pose for in 1954, all smiles and dimples and inflated arms; sitting on no-one's knee but alone, my legs stretched out straight before me, on the photographer's floor; looking not at the camera but at something over to my right, a fluffy mass that somebody is waving, like distant semaphore, to distract my attention.

All smiles, all pride and joy. Never, ever, seeing what is coming.

## *2*

## *Gods and Eyebrows*

I enter Wilford church for the first time at my christening, a tight bud of a baby sleeping in the white shawl my mother has wrapped around me. Outside it is July, and the long slips of willow leaves trail in the sluggish Trent; inside it is cold, cold as the name of Wilford's patron saint Wilfrid, the holy man who baptized heathens in the river. Even within the walls of the church, river-damp rises from the flags around the font; my mother shifts her feet slightly, as if she feels it rising through the soles of her shoes. Behind our family group the choir processes into church, the wooden cross bobbing above the four-cornered hats of the choristers, their long dark robes gliding bodiless between the pews. The cross dips to pass beneath the pierced screen between nave and choir and moves into the stalls below the east window. And, up in the window, the Wilford Jesus looks down upon the service, sturdy and strong in his rose-pink robe of glass, the evening light shining on his broad calm face.

*Yesterday*, the parish magazine will report, *we had our second public baptism. Roberta Jean played her part well, and never made a murmur. That is, perhaps, a slight exaggeration, for she made one valiant attempt to join in the Magnificat, but finding the setting not to her liking gave up the venture; she was a model child.*

20

It is just the one cry I give, a yell bursting out from the tight muffling silence, as the choir begins the sung Magnificat: *My soul doth magnify the Lord.*

*Hush*, my mother says, rocking me gently, and I subside.

As we emerge at the church door my grandfather takes a photograph. A dark photograph, except for the vicar's white cassock as he stands to my mother's left, and a half-moon of my face peeping from the pale blanket. Elsewhere the picture is dark and sombre: the stone of the church porch distempered with soot from the power station, my mother's dark suit, her dark gloved hands with the fingers spread against the blanket as she holds me tightly, her dark hat relieved only by a band of marguerites.

My mother is not smiling, although this is a joyous occasion. She does not look at the camera, or the child in her arms. She peers heavy-eyed out into the daylight, her eyes blank behind their pale spectacles, as if turned inward on something no one else can see: God, perhaps, who, she will tell me, is close by, all around us, everywhere. Just invisible, out of our sight.

Much later, as I grow into words, finding first my voice and then my feet, I will go back and back into church at my mother's side, but I do not find him. The cross, the choristers, the rosy Jesus: all these I can see, can believe in. But not my mother's God, who, because he cannot be everywhere, must be somewhere, hiding behind the pews or concealed by the dark red curtain at the foot of the belltower; a sneaky God, creeping up behind me to frighten me, to find me out in doing wrong. And at some point during my early years I decide I will not have this immortal being for a deity: ineffable, invisible, hid from my eyes. Instead I will have a God I can see, whose approach I can hear, who is outside, who comes openly into my world. At home, playing in my garden at the foot of the railway bank, I find him.

For the first seven years of my life we live in a rented house on Vernon Avenue, a 1930s end terrace with a small front garden and a rear garden that backs straight on to the railway embankment. Every working day my father buttons his grey gabardine and trudges across the Toll Bridge for the bus into town and his job at the GPO; my mother stays at home with me, baking and washing, taking me down to the riverbank where we fish for stickleback and cut stems of pussy willow to bring home and watch the furred buds break into the curled green fingers of leaves. I am an only child, and in my early years an only child feels like a good thing to be, a wonderful thing. I have a specialness, a place at the centre of things that I will cling to long after it has ceased to do me good. For now, I am too much myself to feel loneliness, but loneliness is there, waiting in the darkness for its moment, like the shadow on a lung. As a child, when I find myself too much alone, I sing. I sing hymns, and the songs that Uncle Mac plays on Saturday mornings on the Light programme. My current favourite is Tommy Steele's *Little White Bull,* which I like because there is a story in it, a story with a happy ending. I am a great singer, on the trolleybus, in town, but most of all in my back garden or sitting on the kitchen step, waiting for the trains and playing with my ball.

When I hear a train coming in the daytime I run into the back garden to stand by the fence and watch the long slow line of maroon carriages go by. Or, if not carriages, open trucks with sand or gravel for the brickworks up at Ruddington, next stop along the line.

Or coal. There is still coal, lots of it, in those days.

As the train passes, I listen to the slow, familiar four-part beat of wheels on rails, duh-duh-duh-*dur*, duh-duh-duh-*dur*. I stand very still, because God is coming, and God will come last, when the rest of the train has passed by. At the end of every train there is a brown truck, like a shed on wheels, where the guard lives. The shed has doors, at both front and back ends, and a small platform with a rail around it outside each door, so that the guard can stand and look out or merely lean on the rail and watch the world go by. He has a black uniform and a black cap with a glossy peak and when I see him leaning out I wave, and he smiles and waves back, the slope of the grassy bank between us, him looking down and I looking up. When he waves, I am proud. I know he can see that I am a good child, not like the boys from the Deering who scramble up the bank and throw stones at the trains, or fling showers of gravel down into our gardens, dirty boys who laugh and run when any watchful parent appears. I am small, in my gingham dress, but I understand the rules of the world, the way of things. The embankment is the border of my territory, its shiny level rails gleaming above me like the horizon of another world, the dark lines of telegraph wires strung out along the border to signal the danger, to remind me that on the other side of the embankment is wilderness.

The train recedes. It leaves a burning smell, a grey tattered trail of smoke floating above the embankment, a fading vibration in the ground. And a soft fall of black cinders tumbling down the bank, cinders that will run out onto the back lane, carpeting it with dark snow.

And on Sunday, when Mr Schofield says Let us pray, I know that God does not look like the white-bearded old man in the Sunday schoolbook illustration, the picture copied from the Sistine Chapel ceiling: an angry God, pointing from the sky with his cloudy finger and visiting plagues and famines on the sinners below. I know that God is the guard on the train; a smiling God, who is pleased with me.

In this smiling world I am, almost exclusively, a happy child. There is no anger in my home, only my parents' love: a quiet, gentle kind of love, soft to the touch, like the willow buds in the vase on the kitchen table. Occasionally, if I am naughty, my mother will reprimand me, but she lays her hand, and her words, gently on me. She does not shout, my father does not shout. When I have gone to bed each night my parents sit downstairs in silence, my father smoking a last cigarette before coming to bed, whistling the smoke into the air; my mother sewing. Only the radio talks, and if there is shouting on the radio my mother will put down her sewing, get up and turn the dial to the Third programme, smoothing the sharp voices into music. And

I shut my eyes and prepare to sleep, content for the God of the night train to pass me by in the dark.

The anger in my world, when finally it begins to emerge, comes from an unexpected place.

While I am still very small, my Granny and Grandpa Bailey buy me the first present I can remember, a teddy bear. The fur of this teddy bear is not golden but black and creamy white; he has black arms and legs and black ears, but a white face and body. He is not a teddy bear but a panda, and this new word, a perfect fit for a child's voice, becomes his name. Only when presented with my panda, I cry, which upsets Granny and Grandpa terribly.

My mother gets up and takes hold of Panda by his outstretched arms. She looks into his face with its dark snout and heavy eyebrows, strips of dark fur fabric tacked above his brown button eyes.

I think it's the eyebrows, she says. They make him look as if he's frowning.

My mother lays Panda down on her knee, gets out her sewing box and snips the eyebrows away. I stop crying and watch as the dark strips fall to my mother's knee. They shift against her cotton skirt and arch their backs like the caterpillars in the garden. I put out my hand. Panda, no longer frowning, is returned to me.

It is a curious thing: but eyebrows run in our family. And not just in my mother's family, the Baileys, with their bushy and undisciplined eyebrows, the hairs tough as tussock grass in delicate skin; but also in the Plumbs, whose dark colouring means that eyebrows are the dominant feature of the face, not malign but definite, thick brush-strokes above subordinate eyes. I, too, inherit them, although the Bailey element in my genetic makeup leaves my eyebrows lighter, mid-brown to mouse, and the bushiness is of no concern to me until the age of plucking arrives. My Grandpa Bailey's brows have already turned white by the time I am born, and although people who do not know him think he has a rather fearsome appearance, this is mostly due to the round dark glasses he wears to protect the weakness of his eyes. My Grandpa Bailey plays on an old upright piano while I sing, he has a voice that sounds like the crunching of warm gravel, on Sunday afternoons there is always a small present for me hidden in the shelves of his bureau. I love him with a fierceness and devotion that my Plumb relations will never inspire.

My father's eyebrows, though, like those of his siblings and most of my Plumb cousins, are true black. Not angry, not frowning, simply black.

As black, but not as thick, as the brows of Mike Mercury.

At number 30, like most of our neighbours, we have no television. When the decade turns, though, we acquire a set, a Bush with an art deco bakelite cabinet and a small fat screen. The first pictures I see, after the set has warmed up, are the faint black forms of horses running across a grey mottled background. I take to westerns like *Wagon Train* and *Laramie*; there seems to be little else on. But when Gerry Anderson's puppet series begin to occupy the teatime schedules, I am hooked. These shows are set in the future, where spaceships are commonplace, where buildings can rise

27

up out of the ground and sink back into it when threatened by the forces of evil, and where each futuristic vehicle is captained by a dashing and handsome pilot with a name to match, a kind of sci-fi Mills and Boon hero: Mike Mercury, Steve Zodiac, Troy Tempest. With each of these I am in love, in turn. Not all my heroes are dark: Steve Zodiac is a blond bombshell with an adoring (blonde) sidekick, Dr Venus; what they all have in common, apart from their strings, is luxuriant, beetling eyebrows. Unlike Panda, though, they do not frown. Their wooden faces are sculpted into permanent smiles, smiles that persist through dangerous missions and encounters with unsmiling, foreign villains. Smiles that are a tight upward curve of their polished lips. Smiles that prevail over evil, set in stories where the good end happily, the bad unhappily. At teatime, my appetite for my Hovis sandwiches is no longer what it was. I am in love.

My first impulse is to communicate how I feel, but I restrict this need to my parents. I begin to protect myself, instinctively, from my friends.

At Wilford School, other names and faces are beginning to interest the girls moving out of infant classes into juniors. Diane Wing brings a photo into class, and tells us it is of Cliff Richard; soon it will be the Beatles. I scrutinize the photo, but the face is not quite right. There is a lack of definition in Cliff's cheerful grin, something lightweight, pleasing and yet foolish. I am polite and guarded about my own affections. I keep at home my comics with their heavy line drawings of the crew of *Stingray* and its black-browed captain; I am already painfully sensitive to unkind laughter, and jeers about puppets. Not until the Monkees' Davy Jones is causing girls to swoon will any flesh and blood idol fulfil my requirements of good looks and eyebrows. Troy Tempest will be succeeded in due course by Scott Tracy, and nothing has changed.

Downstairs, the black and white TV flickers its Morse code in the living room; upstairs, in the cold of my bedroom, Panda is still there, forgotten for now, on a shelf above the bed. Without his eyebrows he looks forlorn, his mouth an upturned V, his empty arms held out at his sides. A sad look in his brown button eyes, as if he is remembering the anger my mother snipped away. But I have forgotten what Panda's eyebrows looked like, I have no need of his anger. There is anger somewhere in the room, though, floating invisible in the faintly gritty air; waiting to be remembered.

## 3

### *Swan*

My second favourite song is sung by Danny Kaye. It is called *The Ugly Duckling.* It is a sad song which ends happily. The poor duckling is driven away by the other birds, and hides from them through the winter. In the spring, when she emerges from her hiding-place among the reeds, the birds see that she is a swan, and they take her back. I know the song by heart, and I can sing it word-perfect from the beginning to the end. Only when I sing the sad words about the duckling's loneliness, there is something in them that I recognize. This something is truth. The sad words haunt me, they belong to me in a way that the happy ending does not. So mostly I only sing the ending when the guard has waved to me, when I am feeling happy.

But the ending does not take away the picture of the duckling in my mind. She is still there, frightened, shivering, cowering lonely in the reeds through the grey cold winter. I cannot forget her, I cannot abandon her for the swan.

And then, one Saturday during the long hot summer of 1959, something wonderful happens. There is a swan in my back garden, a real live swan.

I know about swans. As a child living close to the river, I often see them at the foot of the steps below the Victoria Embankment, jostling the ducks for titbits, stretching out their white curved necks for bits of bread.

30

These swans are mute swans, *mute* meaning that they have no song. Perhaps because they cannot sing, they do not look like the other breeds that are more like large ducks; they have stern faces with black brows jutting over orange beaks. The boys on the avenue say that a single strike from their wings can kill a man, but they like telling me things that will frighten me. I do not believe them, not quite.

But this swan is in my back garden, her wings held open like huge cupped hands, padding around on her great black feet and nibbling at the grass. She is so large the lawn beneath her feet looks tiny, like the square green rug in my bedroom. I take a step towards her, and then I stop. I turn and go back into the kitchen, where my mother is washing clothes in the sink.

Mummy, I say, There's a swan in the garden.

My mother is not looking towards the garden. She is looking out of the kitchen window at the side of the house, gazing down the avenue while she wrings out a check shirt of my father's into a sausage between her hands. There is a dark wet patch on her apron where the water has splashed over the edge of the sink.

Is there? she says, and carries on with her washing. The shirt drips a trail of soapy water from the thick green bar of Fairy which is beside her, coated in sparkling bubbles, on the wooden draining-board.

I wait, to see if she is going to come and have a look. Then I go back out into the garden, to see if the swan is still there.

She is still padding about, but now her wings are folded back into her body. When she sees me she opens

31

her dark beak and hisses. Not a whistle, as it says in the song, but a hiss, like the sound of the gas fire coming on in the morning. I am not frightened, just curious, and interested.

I go back inside again.

It's still there, I say.

By this time my mother has piled her washing into a wicker basket, ready for pegging out. She follows me out into the garden, and sees the swan.

Oh, she says, There really is one.

Instead of pegging out the washing, she takes the bowl back inside, and calls me in. She is taking off her apron and finding her handbag.

We have to go down to the phone box, she says.

I go into the phone box with her while she makes the call. It is tight in the phone box, but I do not know how to use it. There is a button A and a button B, which confuse me. My mother dials the numbers, one after the other, the silver dial turning to the right and then turning back with each number. Each number has letters around it. I know all my letters, and I say them to myself, quietly, while my mother speaks into the receiver.

After my mother has made the call, we walk back up the avenue and wait. The swan waits with us, unfolding her wings and folding them up again. I look at the S of her neck, the dark head at the end of it, and think how tiring it must be, to have such a long neck, what hard work it must be for the swan to hold up her head.

She does not hiss again until the man comes.

He comes in a van, and has long leather gloves and a kind of shepherd's crook with a sharp end to it which he uses to get hold of the swan by her neck. My mother tells me to go and play indoors for a while, but I only go as far as the side of the house and sit down on the back doorstep, squeezing my hands together and praying that a train will come, that God will appear and make sure that the swan's neck is not broken. I wait, and say my prayer again, but there is no train. All I can hear is the swish of the swan's wings, like the sound of the washing flapping in the breeze. Finally the man comes round the corner of the house. He has his arms around the swan's body and is holding her in a kind of sack, with her black feet dangling. When he sees me on the step he strokes her neck and says to me

She couldn't take off, you see. Your garden's too small for her.

When my father comes home, I hear my mother telling him about the swan. And there really was a swan, she says, laughing a little, not unkindly, but gently, the way she does most things. But her voice sounds surprised. And I don't understand why she didn't know that I was telling the truth, why she thought it was just one of my stories.

Will the swan be all right now? I ask my mother as she switches on my nightlight with the pink shade, and I am sure she says, Of course.

I want to know if the swan had a happy ending. But when she is gone, I feel the sadness of the duckling again.

One cool day at the end of autumn, we are sitting on the trolleybus going down Wilford Road on the way into town, as we often do. Sometimes we don't get the bus but do our shopping in the shops on Wilford Road. I like going into Mr Auckland's and smelling the sweet smell of the meat that hangs on hooks in the back of the shop, out of sight, I like seeing the waves and hollows in the thick wooden table where he cuts up our chops. But being on the bus is best, because on the bus I can sing. The number 40 rolls quietly along the road, the ladder on its roof striking blue sparks as it moves from one set of overhead wires to the next. I sit next to the window, while my mother sits beside me in her smart mac and best gloves and her silk headscarf with the butterflies on it, knotted underneath her chin to protect her ears and neck from the wind. On her knee she has the small blue suitcase she always takes to Scarborough. I look at the suitcase, but I don't ask why she has brought it; I am too busy singing. When the bus is moving, I sing; when it stops, I stop too. A lady on the seat in front of us turns round and smiles at me and tells me I will make it rain.

I explain to the lady that it's not me doing the singing, that it's a kind of radio on the bus which starts up when the bus is moving.

Oh, she says, smiling at my mother, I see.

I know when the lady looks at my mother that she doesn't believe me. I like it when other people believe my stories, but I know my stories are just stories, just the blue sparks in my head; they are not like lies that would make me a bad girl in the eyes of God.

There is a different kind of lie, and I am about to find it out. It is a lie that is afraid of its own badness, so it is silent. It is not a lie you tell, but a truth you do not tell.

The bus reaches the Market Square, and we get off outside Griffin and Spalding, the biggest department store in town. Sometimes we take the lift to the top floor to meet Granny Bailey and all the ladies with hats for tea and cakes in the Terrace Restaurant. But today we turn and go up Market Street, past the theatre and onto Goldsmith Street, turning left into a small road with trees growing along its pavements called Chaucer Street. There is a high, red-brick building on our right with a sign over its door. The sign has the words Ear and Nose and some other words on it, and we go inside.

There is a huge hall with a high ceiling and lights hanging down on long cords. The floor is covered with grey shiny lino, and I walk very carefully so as not to slip. A lady walks across the floor in black shoes with hard heels that make a noise. My mother's shoes are brown and quiet. Brown with soft sides, so you can squash them with your hands.

My mother speaks to a lady sitting at a desk, and hands the suitcase to her across the desk. The lady puts it down, and we are asked to wait. We wait in the hall, sitting on old high-backed chairs like the dining chairs at home. My mother gives me a copy of *Playhour* to read, but today I do not want to read, I want to know what is happening. Something is happening around me, and I don't know what it is.

35

The lady at the desk calls us in to an office. In the office a man in a suit like my father's sits behind a polished wooden desk with a red leather top and a row of pens that stick out of the top like knives. He gets up, shakes hands with my mother, and offers her a chair.

I stand up, between them, in front of the desk, while the man talks to my mother. In their conversation, I hear some words I have only ever heard in Dr Clarke's surgery, adenoids and tonsils. If you have adenoids, you talk as if your nose is bunged up, but everybody has tonsils. I have seen my tonsils, by opening my mouth very wide and looking in a mirror. They are like red front teeth, in two hollows at the very back of your mouth, so that it looks as if there is another mouth behind the one you use to speak.

The man gets up and smiles at me. He tells me that I will have to stay for a few days at the clinic, at Chaucer Street, because I have to have my tonsils out.

I look at my mother, who is still sitting down. I think she says I will be coming home on Saturday.

Then she gives me a kiss, and leaves me there.


The first night on the ward I pray very hard. I whisper under the bedclothes because we are not allowed to call out. I try to imagine how far we are from Wilford, I hope that the trains will pass the hospital. I listen carefully and sometimes I hear a whistle, faintly in the distance. I promise to be good if only my mother will come back for me in the morning.

In the morning, when a nurse wakes me, I ask if she has come.

Oh, no, she says. No parents allowed while we're on the ward.

Will she come back on Saturday? I say.

I suppose so, she says. If you behave yourself.

When she walks away her shoes squeak on the lino.

While I am on the ward, I do not try to tell myself stories. Like *Playhour* I understand they are of no use to me here. I sit up in bed and take in my surroundings. The ward is large and circular with the beds arranged around its walls, leaving a wide space of lino in the centre. The nurses walk to and fro across the centre carrying doses of medicine and metal trays covered with flannels; they have black lace-up shoes and Royal blue nylon dresses. The very small children are in cots, but I have a real bed with no rails around it. To my right is a little boy referred to by the nurses as number three; I am number four, the numbering beginning with the children to my right and working its way clockwise around the ward. I talk to the little boy, and he stands up at the rail of his cot in his stripy pyjamas and tells me that his name is David. I remember to behave myself; I do not cry or scream or demand my mother. I sleep in my bed, say please and thankyou like the good child I am.

But on the first morning I do something wrong. For breakfast, we are given thick triangular slices of white toast spread with Golden Shred. When I get my toast, I hand it back, and ask to have my marmalade with the pieces of peel taken out of it, the way my mother does at home.

The nurse who brings the breakfasts stares at me, but she goes away and brings me a new piece of toast. I examine it. In the clear golden jelly there are still two dark orange strands of peel.

Can you take them out, please? I ask, pointing to the strands. I am still very polite.

The woman snatches my toast away again and strides across the ward, announcing to everyone within earshot that number four is a spoilt brat.

I don't know what I have done wrong. I only know that the nurse does not like me.

On the day of the operation, all the children are taken from their beds to a room where there is carpet on the floor. We sit wearing our dressing gowns on the carpet, play with the soft toys piled in a box on the floor, and wait for our numbers to be called. When it is my turn, I am taken to another room where lots of people are standing around a bed. I have to lie down on the bed, and they gather round and look at me. When I wake up, I am back in my bed on the ward. The nurse who does not like me brings a plastic bowl, and I am sick, red sick into the bowl. This time, I ask for my mother, but the nurse says that she is not allowed to come until Saturday, when if I am well enough I can go home.

The next morning I have a very bad sore throat and it hurts to talk. I lie on my side so that I can whisper to David, and he lies on his side and shakes his head behind the bars of the cot to say he cannot hear me. When I turn my head I can see the nurses going through the swing doors to fetch the breakfasts and I think of the orange peel scratching my throat. But today it is porridge for breakfast, thick grey lumps of oatmeal which make me feel like being sick again. Only I must try very hard not to be sick, because if I am sick again I may not be allowed to go home.

When the nurse comes for my bowl and bends down to the bed, I whisper to her. I can't hear you, she says, so I whisper again. She too shakes her head and takes the bowl to a woman in a check overall who is pushing a trolley around the ward, rattling loudly with the spoons and the crockery and metal wheels.

Number four wants some writing paper, says the nurse. What on earth does she want writing paper for?

The woman with the trolley looks across at me. I have taken my right hand out of the bedclothes, with the tips of my fingers held against my thumb. I am making a bird's-face hand, the hand my mother tells me to make when I hold a pencil.

The trolley woman laughs. She wants to draw, Dora.

But I do not want to draw. I am going to write a letter, the first letter I have ever written, to my mother.

I am given a stumpy pencil and a lined piece of paper torn out of a book, with a proper book to rest it on. My hand feels soft and twitchy, but I try hard to make my letters stand straight. By dinner time, the letter is finished.

*Daer Mummy I*
*am a lot betu.*

*But I will be*
*comming home on*
*SaturDay. Loue*
*from Roberta*
*Plumb.*

The next time the nurse comes for my bowl, I hand her the letter, folded over in the centre to keep the words private, and ask for it to be posted to my mother. Then I wait quietly, pulling the bedclothes up around my throat, watching the half-window in the door leading from the ward.

When my mother reappears on Saturday to take me home I am already dressed, sitting in a chair beside my bed with the blue suitcase beside the chair, and smiling again. My mother is smiling too, and she has my letter in her hand. She hugs me and says What a brave, clever girl, and I am glad that she is proud of me.

But in the taxi going home I do not sing. I tie knots in my handkerchief and look out of the window at my smeared reflection. My smile will not hold still, my face wants to fold and cry. There is an odd feeling in my throat, as if something is lodged there, something that must have been left behind after the operation, stuck in the hollow where my tonsils used to be. I try to talk around the obstruction but my words come out thin and shaky, as if they have squeezed themselves past other words. When my mother asks me if I am all right my *Yes* is faint and lifeless. My mother looks at me, but she does not ask again. At home she sits me in the softest chair in the front room and gives me a book to look at while she gets the tea ready.

The book is a very old one, with a soft linen spine. It is my mother's childhood copy of Alice in Wonderland, a beautiful book with come-to-life panorama. I ask if I can colour in the illustrations, and my mother says, Of course you can, and brings my crayons. When she comes back to say that tea is ready, I have drawn pictures on the blank pages of the book, and on the white spaces of the pages with writing on them. I have drawn the church and the cross and the choristers, giving them red and green and purple gowns topped with diamond-shaped hats. And I have drawn the characters from the book: Alice, in her flowery dress, and the furious Queen of Hearts, who is always shouting *Off with his head!,* the Red Queen in her flowing robes and stiff bonnet, its starched white wings curving out at the sides of her scowling face.

My mother looks over my shoulder.

There's fancy dress at the Rectory Garden Party next week, she says. If you're feeling better, would you like to go as Alice?

I look again at the picture of the Red Queen. I cannot shout, but I like the idea of the shouting, of freeing the words that are trapped in my throat. I like the idea of having my voice back.

I shake my head. I want to go as the Red Queen.

For the next four nights my mother labours over the costume on her Singer, treadling her way through the seams of the white dress with its red felt hearts,

41

handstitching the red cloak with its bell sleeves and guards of cottonwool ermine, and the taffeta of the stiff winged bonnet.

At the Rectory Garden Party my mother takes a photograph of me, solemn in my regal robes. I would like to shout out *Off with their heads!* at the groups of screeching children running round the lawn and over the Rector's flowerbeds, but when I try my voice is still too weak. What I can manage, though, is the Red Queen's scowl, from beneath her heavy bonnet: an uncertain, unaccustomed frown, running from my lowered eyebrows to my tight pinned mouth; a wisp of anger scudding across my face as I look back at my mother.

## *4*

## *The Dramp Club*

As the swing swoops forward I grip the cold chains in my fists, lean back and stretch my legs out in front of me, until they are held out horizontal. As I go up, my toes point first towards the French windows, then the upstairs windows, then the capital X of the TV aerial on the roof. I come down, and the house rises above my feet until I am close to the ground, braking the swing with a scrape of my feet on my father's new lawn. The chains grate against the bridge of the frame as I stop. Then a new song starts to shape itself around my voice, and I kick off again.

I am singing again, but I do not sing *The Ugly Duckling* any more. My songs are made up now, they come from the same place in my head as the stories. They are happy songs, without the duckling's sadness or the Red Queen's frown. And it is summer, 1962, and a good song.

> *Oh, wonderful day;*
> *Oh, marvellous day;*
> *Singing oh-I-oh-I-oh-I-ay,*
> *Singing oh-I-oh-I-oh-I-ay.*

Through the thin screen of rosebush hedge to my left I can see our new neighbour Mary gardening, planting a plant with long green stems and long white

43

buds in her crowded flowerbed. Mary is thin, like the hedge, but kind, and she is in love with Wordsworth. She sometimes talks to herself, which my mother says is because she is a writer, but she also talks to me. You'll make it rain, she says. But I am already moving, curling my legs under me on the backswing and stretching them out, feeling them pushing into free air as I move forward.

*Oh, wonderful day;*

My song is a simple one, but it is mine. Like the lawn, the apple trees, the hedge, the French windows, the swing with its long straight legs hammered firmly into the ground with four metal hoops. And our new house and garden: a garden with space enough for the invisible arc drawn by the swing in the air; and space enough for the long line of washing that runs the length of the garden, swaying on two tall wooden props, sheets pegged firmly to the line but blowing and flapping in the wind like great white wings.

We have not moved very far. Two doors down from number 30, but no more rent to pay, not ever. My father explains that a mortgage is money paid to yourself, that one day we will have paid the whole two thousand pounds and when that happens we will have a deed that says number 26 is ours for ever. He sits in his new armchair with a packet of Park Drive and his matches beside him on the wooden shoebox and smiles the broad smile which stretches right across his face. In the evenings my mother goes down to the Village Hall for the W.I., or the Young Wives, or the Drama, but as soon as she is back my father goes out to the Ferry Inn. At nine o'clock I watch him take his brown shiny shoes from the box, remove his slippers and change into his outdoor shoes. He checks the clock, takes his gabardine from the coathooks in the hall, and goes off down the avenue for his three pints of Mixed, served in his own silver tankard. He is a homeowner now.

And what a home it is. Two front gates, not one, and a porch with brick tiles all around it to shelter in while you wait for the door to be answered. The front door has long thin stained-glass windows that shine in the evening like the windows in the church. Number 26 is an extended semi, so it is spacious. Upstairs there are three large bedrooms, one over the built-in garage, and a landing where my mother can keep her piano. The garage, where we keep our bikes, is huge, with a concrete floor and a coal-hole at the end nearest the kitchen. When my friends come round, they dare me to climb over the half-height door into the sooty space of the coal-hole, and I grab onto the walls at either side, get my feet up on the door, and lower myself in. The coke crunches under my feet with a noise like a spoon digging into cornflakes.

I do not stay in the coal-hole long. I might sink down into the coke and never get out. I scramble out over the door and pieces of the coke follow me back into the garage, pieces that are not hard and slaty like the old coal but brittle and hollow, like bits of hard black

45

sponge. My mother comes out of the kitchen, looks at my feet, and tells me it is time for dinner. My friends hang around for a while, climbing on the gate and tying a skipping-rope around the gatepost and shouting Giddyup, but there is no invitation.

For the first summer our back garden is as the Watsons left it. Mr Watson was old and ill and past gardening, and Mrs Watson could only manage cutting back the clumps of aubretia and stonecrop in the rockery. Beyond the steps down from the rockery, when we first move in, there is a wilderness. The garden faces south, but it is dark and damp, overhung by nettled flowerbeds and unpruned apple trees whose tired branches lean on the long grass. There are sticky treetrunks to climb and thorny bushes to hide behind with green hairy gooseberries among their spikes, white stones to unearth and objects half-buried in the soil. Underneath one of the stones is a seashell the size of my hand that shines with the colours of petrol on water. The mouth of the shell has a piece broken off and the long flute is cracked, but when I hold it to my head it still has the sea in it.

And there is a plum tree. A plum for the Plumbs, my father says. He starts to plan the lawn, and the concrete path which will go right round the garden.

While I am exploring, I hear a train. The slow heavy thump of the wheels means it is a goods, so I have time to scramble down from the upper branches of the Bramley and run back up the garden steps to the rockery before the grey trucks have all passed, while the guard's van is still crossing the bridge above the back lane. I stand in front of the French windows and wave my hand, but I am further away from the railway line than I was at number 30. Our new hedges are high and wild, and next door's garden is now between us and the embankment. The guard is leaning on the rail of the van with his back to me, looking over his left shoulder to the postage-stamp of lawn where I used to be.

I lower my hand. Next time, I will bring a hanky to wave, and he will see the white fluttering movement above the trees and spot me. He will work out that I have moved, and look over to see me at the right time.

Only if he really is God, he should have known already.

My friends Peter and Anthony have called for me, and we are off to the Willowwoods. The Willowwoods are in the eastern half of the Wilford isthmus, on the far side of the railway line, and to reach them we go to the end of Coronation Avenue, underneath the railway bridge, and up the floodbank on the other side. The tarmac path on the crest of the bank goes all the way to West Bridgford, but today we ignore the path and scramble down the tussocky grass on the river side of the floodbank to make our way into the Willowwoods, following the sandy track that heads for the river with the railway embankment on our left. It is August, and the grass is tall and dry with the green bleached out of it, with purple spikes of fireweed that seed clouds of white fluff into the air, fluff that attaches itself to our socks and jumpers. Anthony has a stick, and

47

he swings it around in semi-circles in front of him, slicing off the tops of the nettles. In a few minutes we come out at Clearways Clearing, where the grass is flattened and three paths go off in different directions, narrow trodden grooves in the tall stands of reed and grass and willow saplings.

Peter wants to know where we are going.

The dramp, I say, and Anthony dashes off along the path to the left so as to be there first.

Peter stops to pull his socks up and looks back along the path.

There's that girl from across the bridge, he says, pointing to the head and shoulders just appearing above the floodbank. Shall we wait for her?

I am looking round in the undergrowth for a stick for myself, one strong enough for the work we have to do at the dramp. Willow branches are too bendy, the best kind of stick is a piece of firewood dropped by the night fishermen.

No, I say. She'll catch us up.

We head off to the left, following Anthony. Ahead of us the earth embankment comes to an end a hundred yards short of the river, and the viaduct begins. A line of high blue-brick arches leads out towards the Trent, the first supports of the bridge that carries the railway over the water into the city. Beneath the arches it is dark and damp and cool. Nothing grows in the loose stony soil under the spans of the bridge, but pools of water collect in the hollows in the ground, fed by thin waterspouts like toilet overflows high up, where the arches meet the spans of the bridge. The water pings and trickles and the pools spread outward, seeping through the smaller arches cut through the piers, little arches the size of doorways that connect one brick chamber with the next. The task of all dramp members – solemnly sworn beneath the doorway arches of the viaduct, with names marked in chalk on the blue-brick piers – is to prevent these pools of water from becoming lakes, from rising into flood and inundating both Willowwoods and village.

Anthony is at work already, carving out drainage channels from one of the pools with the end of his stick, letting the water run and seep away into the undergrowth of the Willowwoods. I set off through the doorway arch into the next chamber. Either side of me there is an opening to the sunny outside, but in front and behind me the dark pier walls stretch the full width of the bridge, with only the doorway arches to keep me in touch with the others. I hear Anthony laughing, and Peter's voice, and then a girl's voice, calling out, cutting into the echo.

Anthony is shouting. I can't hear what he says, but then the ground rumbles, and the water in the pools bounces, sending up little jerky splashes, as a train approaches along the embankment above us. As the engine reaches the viaduct the hard clanging of the wheels comes down the arches straight into the ground, goes right through the soles of my sandals and back up my legs all the way to my ears. And the smoke billows down in speckled ashy clouds and drifts in to the sides of the dramp through the blue-brick arches.

The clanging stops. The train is off the bridge and puffing through the Meadows on the way to the

Victoria Station. The ponded water settles and I look round for my stick.

*Boo!* says the girl, right in front of me. I jump and she grins. She has her hair tied back in a ponytail, but the short bits nearest to her face stick up around her head like curly wires. She has a yellow cardigan and skirt on, the skirt being one of her mother's rolled up around the waist. And no stick, because she is not a member of the Dramp Club.

You're all dirty, she says, pointing at my face. I touch my cheek and my hand comes away with black fingerprints on it.

She looks at the ends of my fingers.

That's what criminals' hands look like, she says. Your Mum will think you've been arrested and taken to the Police Station.

I wipe my hand on my shorts.

You shouldn't be here, I say. You're not a member.

Did you see the man? she says. I shake my head and she points back out towards the Willowwoods, close to the river where the saplings grow taller and their branches hang down into the water.

I saw him, she says. He had a long brown coat on with spit down it and he said he had something to show me.

Tell her what it was, says Anthony, putting his crewcut head around the doorway.

The girl undoes the buttons of her cardigan and shows her stomach.

He did this, she says. He had no clothes on under

50

his coat, so I could see his tail.

I trace an arc around where I'm standing with my stick. Then I start to make practice grooves in the soil, rehearsing for the work to come.

Men don't have tails, I say. You're telling lies.

The girl laughs. Then Anthony laughs as well, and Peter goes back through the doorway into the first chamber. I can hear him scraping out a new water channel with his stick.

You're not supposed to be here, I say. I'm Dramp leader and I decide who's allowed in.

The girl starts to rebutton her cardigan.

The Dramp is stupid, she says. It's a stupid kids' game.

I tuck my stick under my arm and walk round her.

Go and have a look then, she says. And you'll see who's telling lies.

I look towards the bank. In the thickest stand of willows, in the space between two branches, there is something brown, or beige, moving, or flapping in the wind.

I dare you, she says, giving me a push. I stumble forward a few paces, and stop. I am frightened, but it feels as if the fear is behind me.

No, I say. You're a liar.

The girl starts to laugh again. I turn away from her and march off back along the path. When I get back to Clearways Clearing I stop and sit down in the grass. I wait for the others, but I don't know if they're going to come. Then I hear Peter and Anthony coming along the path towards me. They stop and look at me and sit down and after a bit Peter says he has to go home, it's past his dinner time.

Anthony throws his stick into a bed of nettles. Then he starts to pull his grey school socks up.

Don't you know about men and women? he says.

Of course I do, I say. I say it very quiet, the way my mother says things. Then Anthony shuffles towards me on his knees and pushes me down on my back and kisses me. But it is not like my mother's kiss. His mouth is like a big wet hand over my mouth and I can feel the wetness all round my top lip and my chin. My mouth feels as if it is being drowned and I clamp my lips tight shut because there is spit running down them and if I open my mouth I might get a horrible disease. Anthony has a red face and I could catch scarlet fever from him and die. I dig into the ground with my feet, trying to get upright, scraping muddy grooves in the grass.

As soon as he lets me go I jump up and pull my hanky from my pocket and run home as fast as I can without opening my mouth. I go straight upstairs to our new bathroom and wash my face with Cussons Imperial Leather soap, not once but lots of times, and then I wash the taps in case the disease is on them too. When I go downstairs, my mother is in the kitchen draping a pastry lid over a meat pie. Her hands are white and floury and the knuckles on her fingers look like little roses as she holds the pie-dish up to cut off the excess pastry. I sit on the edge of the dining table with my feet on a chair and watch her through the serving hatch. She asks me if I had a nice time and I tell her I think Anthony has scarlet fever, and I'm afraid of catching it and dying. My mother says she had scarlet fever when she was young and she didn't die, and in any case I couldn't catch it from Anthony, he just has a high colour and not a disease.

I get down from the table, and go into the kitchen to help with the pie, and my mother sees the state of my clothes. She makes me show my hands are clean before I am allowed to make a pattern with my thumbs in the pie-crust. When I have finished she smiles at me and says, That's nice. I look at the pie, with its frill all round the outside and the fork-holes in the middle to let the air come out. And I say, Mum, men don't have tails, do they? and she looks at me and says, Who told you that?

A girl from over the bridge, I say. They don't, do they, Mum?

She doesn't answer straight away, because the pie has to go into the oven before the pastry spoils. But I know from the way she's looking down with the Bailey eyebrows raised that the answer is yes.


On the second morning of the new school year I am left to sleep until my red alarm clock says that it is ten past eight. Ten past eight means no school today, it means something bad. Something my mother has not told me about: the dentist, or perhaps even the clinic again. I turn over and sink lower into my feather bed, but it has become all lumps and hollows in the night. And I need to go to the toilet.

My mother and I walk the two miles along the tarmac path on the floodbank to the dental surgery at

West Bridgford. My mother sits on a dining chair at the back of the room and the dentist tells me to open wide and pokes my teeth. There is another man in the surgery, the man who has a gas-mask to send you to sleep while your teeth are taken out. He has a dark skin and white teeth and he smiles. The gas-mask is the colour of liver and smells of rubber and it covers your face, all except your eyes. I scream and scream and the dentist tells me to be quiet, that if I keep on screaming I will have to have my tooth out with no gas, and that will really hurt.

Before I fall asleep, I hear the gas hiss through the mask with a sound like the sea in the shell. I dream of the ponds in the dramp filling up from the overflows on the bridge, I hear the water falling ping, ping, ping and getting deeper and deeper until it covers all the Willowwoods with just the whippy willow branches showing above the flood. The water rises, lapping further up the floodbank till I have to run and tell my mother what is happening, we have to move out before the whole village is flooded and we drown. I run as fast as I can but the man in the beige coat is running after me, the man who has a tail beneath his coat, the man who, when I turn around to see if he is catching me up, has Anthony's face. I bang on our new front door and my mother opens it. She puts a finger to her lips, and tells me not to shout.

When I wake up, there is a little parcel on my lap. It is my tooth, wrapped in a tissue to take home with me. I look inside the tissue and the tooth is clean and not bloody, although I know there must have been blood.

I feel in my mouth with the tip of my tongue. The missing tooth is the one behind the dog tooth. My mother says it is to make room for the others to grow.

As we walk the two miles back along the floodbank the air whistles through the gap in my teeth. I keep my hanky over my nose and mouth. Mostly I look down at the path in front of me but as we get nearer to the dramp I have to turn aside and glance across at the dark line of the viaduct. There is something beneath one of the arches that is not dark, something that catches the light and moves.

I look up at my mother. I want to ask her if she can see what I can see. If there is a man there, hiding in the dramp; if he is a bad man, if I should be afraid of him. I look at her, but I do not speak, I do not take the handkerchief from my mouth. I do not ask, because I think she will say that there is no-one there; and I know that I will not believe her.

At home the lawn in the back garden has been mown, pushed into stripes of light green and darker green by my father, as he walked his push lawnmower up and down. I go outside, and stand by the swing. Already I am forgetting the old garden, and the trees and flowers that had to be cut down for the lawn. Now I prefer the long green rectangle with the concrete edges, the space where I can see all around me, where there is nowhere for anybody to hide and jump out. And I take the chains in my hands and get onto the wooden seat of my swing but I stay close to the ground, my feet scuffing the earth.

# 5

## *Paradise*

The train is pulling in to Bakewell Station. My father is at the carriage door, his arm pressed against the open window, hand on the long brass doorlatch. He watches intently as the slope of tarmac rises into platform, as the platform levels out into horizontal, as the lines of platform and coachwork come together. At his feet is the heavy suitcase from the top of the wardrobe, rigid blue cardboard with white metal piping. My mother waits behind him in the corridor with the small brown case and the bag with our sandwiches and Thermos inside. Granny and Grandpa carry smaller cases; their coats hang over Grandpa's right arm, his curled hand with its smoking cigarette pointing out from the hood of tweed and mackintosh. I am too young yet for a suitcase, so I hold my beige gabardine jacket and my bobble hat and the tickets. The train slides silently to a stop opposite a sandstone wall with a cast-iron awning projecting from it and my father opens the door. Down the hill from the station, we know from last year, there is a tea garden serving Teas with Hovis and sticky cakes. We drag the cases down there to wait for our lift to Monyash.

It is 1964, and my father is smiling his holiday smile. Monyash is his gift to us, a limestone village in the Peak District with a single guest house, terms very reasonable, found in the Farm Holiday Guide. The guest house is kept by Harold and Gladys, who we do not know yet but will become our lifelong friends. Harold's spine was shattered by the vibration of Lancasters in the war, but he can still drive, and tell his stories: stories not only of the war but of life in Derbyshire, stories about lorries driving into snowdrifts on the Snake Pass and tractors pulling them out, stories about old Benjy, who sits on the bench outside the Bull's Head every morning waiting for it to open.

I watch Harold as he talks. He has hornrimmed glasses and dark Brylcreemed hair without a trace of grey. His stories are public, spoken aloud, there are no secrets about them. They are not made up; or, if they are, not made up as my stories are, not made from a place inside his head and written down. Harold's stories are easy, there is no sadness in the centre of them, he laughs often as he tells them. But sometimes, when he is not telling stories he cries, not because of the stories but with the pain in his back; cries publicly, his mouth a sudden O of pain, tears running across the creases of his smile.

I have never seen a grown-up cry. I am in awe of the openness of it.

Today Harold is not crying. He is pipping his horn and calling out a greeting as the brown van swings into Coombs Road, with Teddy barking like mad and jumping back and forth over the passenger seat in front of the van. We abandon what is left of our tea and pile into the van, Granny in the front seat next to Harold and the rest of us perching on the long hard benches built in to the van's side walls, our luggage in the central space between the seats, Teddy still barking and scrabbling and slipping over the cases.

The van climbs out of Bakewell, its engine racing as it makes the top of the first wooded incline on the Monyash road. And the light grows and grows, as if the landscape was lifted up to the light, rising to a high plateau of green fields and white walls, and the curved strips of roads and lanes that lead to a level horizon, and dark copses strung out along the skyline; until the last turning where the road dips at the entrance to the dale, and the spire comes into view, and the first barns of the village.

What I find in Monyash is freedom. I hug all the village dogs, indiscriminately, without fear or fastidiousness. I help Mr Handley, who is also lame, to bring in his six cows from the fields to the shed next door for milking. Most of all I walk, I organize expeditions across the fields to Lathkill Dale with my family, expeditions in which I am invariably the leader, the route-finder. Granny Bailey, who will not stir outside, even in the country, without a proper hat, dislikes cows and has difficulty with mud and stiles and stepping-stones, so I clear her path of curious Friesians and arrange flat stones in stream-beds to ease her passage.

Once we get lost within half a mile of the village, roaming the fields until we spot the spire of Monyash church, unconcerned about anything but missing dinner. My mother has an old Ward Lock map, but it is rarely consulted; we wander over dales and pastures unmolested. All the locals know our hosts and their visitors, and those who do not can usually be talked around by my Grandpa, who sweettalks an elderly farmer in his Landrover while I engage in climbing practice in the farmer's quarry, having scaled the gate and headed straight for an easy rock-face. Perhaps the farmer is impressed by the Bailey eyebrows, but more likely it is the Bailey dignity, the containedness of apparent calm. It does not occur to me that this calm comes at a cost, only that it is in the nature of parents and grandparents to display it.

The clinic has receded; this is another world, where I can run and play without any notion of trespass, any consciousness of boundaries. Other things recede too, for a while, the stiff wooden world of my puppet heroes. I ask Auntie Gladys if I can watch Thunderbirds on the television, but it is the next day's walk now that concerns me more. Life in this breezy upland village, with all its light, simplicity and friendliness, has filled me with a confidence that allows me to live for a time in the world, in the present. Instead of stories, on holiday I write a diary in an orange spiral bound notebook, in varied colours of magic marker, but mostly purple. The diary is full of our expeditions, and the day's entry is read out every evening over the dinner table after the pots have been cleared: *Wednesday, Walked to Taddington (4 miles), came back by the Jarnett. Bilberry tart for dinner. Friday, Auntie Gladys packed us our lunch and Harold drove us to Conksbury. We walked the whole length of Lathkill Dale, had our sandwiches by the weir. Daddy said there was enough food for a week. Mum says the Lathkill is the cleanest river in the country. We both had a drink from the spring where it comes out of the big cave in the hillside. (About 8 miles).* Life is simple and sufficient. I never want it to end.

And my family is happy, it never occurs to me for a minute to doubt it. I feel the solidity of my father's childlike pleasure in the holiday, content to go wherever I decree with his packamac in its plastic pouch and his Army Stores canvas bag on his shoulder, off to the Bull's Head every evening for his three pints of Mixed, while the Baileys stay in and read or talk with Harold and Gladys. By eleven - and I share my parents' room, my single bed against the window wall with the stylized flowers on the wallpaper, and the flower-stems that wind like undiscovered paths - he is asleep and snoring, and I am too tired and happy to be kept long awake.

But my mother's pleasure is quieter, less visible, and therefore somehow less sure. From Grandpa she has inherited not only the Bailey dignity, but also their artistic talents. She plays the piano, she acts, she draws and paints. All these things precede my existence, but most of them I will inherit. Nobody doubts this, least of all me. For our evening walk my mother and I often go down the hill to the broad entrance to Lathkill Dale, here no more than a wide pasture with low outcrops of limestone on either side and grassy shelves between them. On one of these shelves my mother likes to sit and sketch, her watercolour paper taped to a hardboard base, elegantly posed in stretch slacks and white cardigan with one leg bent under her to support the board. For a while, I might join her, but the outdoors takes me away as ever and soon I am scrambling up the escarpment opposite, finding a dark flinty patch of rock in the limestone that I am convinced is a fossil of some importance.

From my own side of the dale, with the Brownie box camera, I take one of my first photographs of my mother. I am new to photography, and the picture is not quite in focus. The bands of limestone slope away from her, but she sits securely enough, her brown quilted anorak beneath her, her hand curved around the pencil. And she is smiling; for the camera, or just smiling, the photo is too blurred to see.

Later I take another photograph, of my mother and father together, which is not blurred. On the left, my mother perches on a limestone boulder, one leg bent, the other straight, her hands clasped in her lap. Her mouth is open in what might be a smile, but round sunglasses like my Grandpa's hide her eyes, and the expression of the mouth is not clear enough to be sure. Next to her my father stands in dark slacks and home-knitted cardigan, the wind ruffling his army haircut. My father always smiles with his mouth closed, the lips stretched tight and wide, but in this photo there is no stretch in them. His eyebrows arch good-humouredly, his eyes squint slightly against the sun. He is not sitting but leaning against a rock, his left hand on his hip and his right arm reaching out to rest on the limestone behind him.

Between my father's right hand and my mother's left elbow there is a space of perhaps a foot. Her body is turned away from him, her face looking straight ahead, to the camera's eye. My father leans inward, towards the space, towards his resting hand; he reaches out, but does not touch. It is as if their own togetherness confuses

61

them, and the doubt is there in their faces, doubt about how best to pose for it.

❙

My mother's pose will come back to me, when it is me in the photograph.

Meanwhile, I sit aloft on my own boulder, cross-legged and comfortable, my smile reaching in to every cell of my body. I am a tomboy in grubby shorts and Aertex shirt, my hair basin-cut and mousy, the brown sweet smell of manure perpetually lingering on my Start-Rite sandals. I will not think of the swan for a long time.

And in 1966, when I am twelve, my mother makes her own holiday gift to us. This gift is Penmaenmawr, a small seaside town on the North Wales coast, held in an arc of mountains that reach down to the sea at the extremities of the town, reached whether by road or rail by tunnels cut through the mountains. The mountain at the west end of the bay is a quarried hump of granite with steep shifting slopes of spoil and an ancient hill-fort on its summit; the lower mountain to the east is a dumpy hill with the profile of a recumbent dog when seen from the Llanfairfechan end of the beach: a dog with a dark sad eye of heather, a wooded ruff of neck, and a stony nose sniffing at the incoming tide. Pen has a thriving industry in granite quarrying, plenty of holiday accommodation, and the best beach in Wales, a long, gently shelving expanse of firm sound sand stretching the five miles from the spoil-heaps to the tip of the dog's wet nose.

My mother knows Pen from childhood visits to a cousin who still lives in Colwyn Bay, a few miles down the coast. When we arrive on the stopping Holyhead train from Llandudno Junction, the place is not new territory, as Monyash was new. My mother knows where everything is. She knows where to catch a bus called the Crimson Rambler, which will take us around the foot of the Green Mountain to the road-loops of the Sychnant Pass, where you can shout across at the Echo Rock and hear your name bounce back at you. She knows about Sambrooks' Tea Gardens, built on the landward side of the pedestrian tunnel that runs underneath the railway, connecting the town with its beach.

On our first visit to Sambrooks', after ordering our ice-creams at the counter, we take our tray through the cafe to a back door that leads beneath a fringe of clematis into the tea-garden beyond, a large circular lawn with a corrugated-iron pergola forming its circumference and a flowerbed with a fountain in its centre. And under the pergola, on sticky dark brown chairs, we sit and eat our Knickerbocker Glories, while the wasps stagger drowsily across the tables and the symphonion plays Daisy, Daisy for as long as the penny in its slot lasts.

Mr Sambrook, junior, is on hand to receive our tray when we return it to the cafe. He looks at my mother closely, nodding and smiling as if retrieving her from memory, and my mother enters easily into conversation, about the weather, the beach and the town, and the way Pen is just as she remembered it.

Mr Sambrook nods again, turning over the two half-crowns my mother has given him before dropping them into the pocket of his overall.

You'll be wanting to sign the petition, then, he says.

My mother looks a question.

Against the road, he says, gesturing back into the tea-garden, back the way we have come.

Spread out on a table below the symphonion, there is a map showing where the new road will go. The map is an aerial view of the coastline with the hills poster-painted in bright green, and a royal blue sea edging up to meet them. The prospective road is a thick line of red paint pushing its way between green and blue,

64

past the headland and running the length of the beach, sundering the town from its seafront. About halfway along the line, the words THIS CAFE are written in bold black capitals beside a thick black arrow. Beside the map is an unused Accounts Book, a pencil on a string lying in the centre of its open pages. A note below the book asks patrons to sign the petition before they leave.

In 1966, still on the drawing-boards of Aberconway Borough Council, the A55 Expressway is a streamlined utopian dream of endless traffic-flow, awaiting funding and quickening into life in the Queen's speech. By 1990 it will be real, a double line of concrete thundering with a sleepless roar of freight that penetrates the empty beach and the dilapidated town.

My mother puts another penny in the symphonion. The vertical grey disc turns slowly, gently, the central rod picking out the tiny oblong punctures of the notes. We listen. And then we sign.


At Pen, for the first time ever on a holiday, we are self-catering. We stay at a large Victorian house on the Conway road, whose upper floors are divided into flats. Flat A is on the second floor, and has two bedrooms and its own facilities; Flats B and C are on the first floor, each consisting of a large bedroom and sitting room with kitchenette. The first floor facilities are reached from two doors on the spacious landing; behind the doors, two long thin rooms, the first a toilet and bathroom with bath and basin, the second a toilet alone, with substantial wooden seat. Each morning, we perform the ritual of opening the door of Flat B a crack, and peering out across the landing; then making a dash for the bathroom, trying the door and finding it locked, tiptoeing back and listening for the high click of the bolt, before trying again.

In Monyash, bathing and hair-washing have been the last thing on my mind. But things are changing. At Pen my hair is no longer basin-cut but has wound out like Tressy's nylon locks from my head to cover the back of my neck and stretch down below my shoulders. The Start-Rite sandals have been succeeded by navy Scholls that echo the colour of my Wrangler cord jeans and jacket; a second Wrangler set, in scarlet, is too good even for the beach. As the rest of me reaches up toward the sun I grow into my once too-big feet. And in the last year of primary school I have finally learned to swim, three froglike strokes in the shallow end of Portland Baths while listening to the Kinks' Sunny Afternoon and watching sunlight sparkling on the water. At last I am ready for the sea.

But in the flat I struggle to sleep. Flat B is on the front of the house, its windows overlooking the Conway Road, a single-carriageway arterial route stretching from the Merseyside to Holyhead. Where the road passes through Pen, the traffic crawls at walking pace all day through the town, making the six-mile bus journey from Pen to Conway an hour's trip. At night the congestion eases and the cars and lorries pick up speed, growling past the house until the small hours. Just outside the house there is a loose manhole cover in the road and the cover tips and settles as the wheels of solitary vehicles strike it. The sound is tuneless, not like the gentle four-beat rhythm of the trains at home but two flat metallic clangs and then a space of silence. I lie in bed, sweating in the silences, waiting for the next clang. Through the gap in the curtains the searchlight beam of headlamps scans the ceiling, sweeping it until I fall into the early doze of dreams.

The daytime traffic is mainly a source of amusement to my father, who regards it as he regards the steaming line of cars queueing on wintry mornings to get across the Toll Bridge. It is the amusement of a man who has never owned a car, and never will. As far as the disturbed nights are concerned, next year we will book Flat C, at the back of the house, and all will be well.

And it is as he says. In 1967 the nighttime traffic is put away, almost out of earshot. But I have learned the habit of sleeplessness, and when it revisits me I can still faintly hear the wheels rolling across the manhole cover, the double clang with the missing beats.

Mrs Anderson, a lady from the Wirral, is in charge of the flatlets. There is also a Mr Anderson, who is lame, like Harold, but does not tell stories. He is seen only when we arrive and depart, when the door downstairs marked Private is open for greetings and payment of the rent. He is a small man with the plump remains of disused strength in his arms and legs, who sits in an old armchair by the back kitchen window, smoking Park Drive and looking out on the yard and the lines of tenants' washing. Another line of houses beyond the yard obscures the sea-view, but the coastal sky is bright and floods the kitchen with the brilliance of projected and reflected light.

I peer in to the private room, watching Mr Anderson blowing wisps of smoke towards the window. I wonder if he is remembering the sea, and whether this is just as good as seeing it, or better. He sees me looking and turns and lifts his hand, the fingers waving independently, like the flickering of submerged seaweed fronds; waving a silent hello, as if I was still a child.

Then the door shuts, and he is gone.

The sea. I like it best when it is rough and foaming, the loud grey waves rolling in with sharp crests ready to break into white. I characterize the waves as Big, or Great, depending on their volume. I stand knee-deep in the swell, letting each wave break against my legs, predicting Greatness for some, and only Bigness for others. The days pass under rushing skies and sharp westerlies full of sand, while I push out into the waves and my mother stands still and straight at the foot of the stones, keeping watch over the tide.

In the evenings, it is the rule at Pen, the tide is out. Evening seas are quiet, lit from the left, as the sun sinks over Anglesey and turns the dark timber uprights of the jetty gold. The jetty hums and shivers as the conveyor belt brings pounded stone down from the mountain to the beach, dripping lines of fine grey dust from the trembling belt onto the sand. The ships arrive for their loads of granite from Scandinavia and Poland and stand off in deep water for the night, their hulls white-black spots on the horizon, waiting for a flow tide to bring the draught they need. I paddle to my ankles in the shallows, the waves shrunk to ripples creeping round my feet, the sun drying the back of my royal blue swimsuit.

The broad banks of sand behind me are scribbled over with the stuttered arcs of footprints, and the shapes of giant hearts with feathered arrows scored through them. Within the hearts are words. Declarations of love, statements of allegiance. *Monkees 4 ever, I love Davy Jones, DTJ for RJP.* I write the words with the sharp end of my square blue spade and run, my bare feet splashing in the leats of water trapped by the hard sandy ribs that surround the banks. Some way in front of me, my mother is busy writing other messages with the end of Grandpa's walking stick: *Monkees are awful, Davy Jones is fat.* I pursue her, yelling and laughing out loud, treading the blasphemies back into the sand. As the game progresses, my affection blossoms, pours into my spine like oil. I straighten, bend, or flex with ease. The words dig deep into the sand, words with flourishes and curlicues. Great Waves no longer knock me from my feet but leave me standing.

My new heartthrob moves centre stage into my dreams and stories, stories of unexpected meetings and romance with a teenage fan called Cathy, a girl with long dark hair and a smart new Mary Quant wardrobe. At the end of the day, as I pull the sheets and heavy bedspread up to my neck, Cathy has just caught Davy's eye at an after-show party. She is wearing a shocking pink mini-dress with orange flowers and matching headband. They are holding hands while the less fortunate girls judder the Hitchhiker on the dancefloor and exchange spiteful gossip behind their hands.

I fall asleep. In the night the tide comes in, rolling dark across the beach, and the granite ships weigh anchor. In the morning the hearts and names have been smoothed away and the sand is clear, waiting for fresh marks.

## 6

## *Gone Away*

By the spring of 1965, the Willowwoods are deserted. Or they seem deserted, from the vantage-point of the floodbank path; the plain is a white expanse of flowering hogweed, spreading from embankment to river like a fall of cumulus and concealing the creases of the old paths in the grass. The Dramp Club has been disbanded: even the word has gone silent, a babyhood sound we do not make any more. The willows are pushing up into adolescence, their springy saplings surfacing from the hogweed, covering up the arches of the dramp and the pools of water and the chalk-marks of our names on the blue brick. It is a place I need not go any more. Cannot go, because the paths have disappeared.

The trains have gone quiet too. Just once I climb over the fence, pass the warning sign and scramble up the railway bank on all fours, keeping my head down to conceal the trespass. Once at the top I crouch by the parapet of the bridge, my head against the rough black surface of the capstone, looking up the track. To my left the rails rule dead-straight lines making for the river. I can see the superstructure of the dramp bridge about a hundred yards away, an open framework of iron ribs arching above the track, like the skeleton of a plant tunnel. I know that beyond the bridge and the goods yard at Queen's Walk the rails go on into the city, tunnelling into the hill of the Lace Market, drilling into the soft grit of Bunter sandstone to run through the blackness beneath Thurland Street and Parliament Street, finally emerging into long beams of sunlight grated through the window-slots of the locomotive sheds of the Victoria Station.

And I know that outside the locked doors of the station there is a sign: *This site has now been acquired from British Railways Board for a major comprehensive development.* In one short year the station will be scoured from the earth, rails sliced from their beds and platforms ground into rubble. In five years blocks of pink concrete will fill most of the crater left by the demolition, except for the narrowing void at the northern end of the site where the stability of the rock is suspect. By 1972 only the redbrick clock tower of the old station will remain, fingering the small airspace between the Lego blocks like an ornamental tombstone, the clocks on each of its four sides ticking round the hours that have passed since the red circle of the station on the map of Nottingham became a dot of white.

I look along the line for a little longer, as if the blunt brown square of a guard's van with a waving figure might appear, propelled by an invisible train along the rails, but the track stays empty, and after a minute's grace I release the rough ashlar of the capstone and slide back down the bank, a fall of cinders hushing at my heels. Behind me the arches of the dramp bridge arch away into the distance, like the ruin of a roofless abbey with the monks gone. Turned out of their sheltered home into the world, as if their God had forsaken them.

It is the last day of the spring term, and I am sitting cross-legged on the floor of the school Assembly Hall with a letter in my hand. I know the import of this letter; Mr Smith has gathered the top class together to explain it to us. The letter will tell us which school we will be going to in September, and the name of the school will depend on whether we have passed the 11-plus or not. Mr Smith says we must not be disappointed if we have failed, that if we go to a Secondary Modern instead of a Grammar school, then that is because it is the right school for us. Mr Smith has given this speech many times, and as I listen and watch the way his hand wanders to his small moustache as he speaks, I see that he does not believe it.

I look at the letter in my hand. Through the envelope window I can see my name written in fountain pen, and above my name the printed words *Parent or Guardian of*. Once outside the school gates, some of the boys open their letters, although they are not supposed to. One boy tears open his envelope and looks at his letter, stuffs it in his pocket and goes and hangs upside down on the metal bars outside school. He's going to the Deering, he says, looking up at the rest of us with his face pushing down on his eyes and his spiky hair brushing the dust. He's going to the Deering, and he doesn't care.

I put my envelope in my satchel and start off for home across the green. The satchel thumps on my back. Thump, thump, thump, like a heart in the wrong place. It is not quite time for the Deering pupils to come out yet, but when they do there will be a mass of children in black uniforms swarming down the floodbank path and under the railway bridge onto Coronation Avenue, pulling leaves off the trees in the gardens and throwing stones at the ponies in the Ferry fields. Most of them will pour across the Toll Bridge back into the Meadows, where they live in houses with no gardens or bathrooms, houses that are already condemned. But a few of them will turn the other way, down the Main Road back into the village, yelling rude words at anyone in the brown and gold uniform of Wilford School and trying to get close enough to shake their heads at you. And to stop them getting close enough, you run, because everyone says their hair has things in it.

When I get home I am out of breath and my heart has found its way round to the front. My chest is thumping so hard I can hear it in my throat. I hand the envelope to my mother and she looks at the window of the envelope and then at me and says, Shall we wait for Daddy?

I do not answer straight away. In the pause it seems to me that there is a moment when things might change, when my mother will take charge of the news inside the envelope, and clearly tell me if it is good or bad. I notice that she is no longer looking at me, but at the envelope in her hand; that it shivers slightly, like a leaf about to fall. And a part of me wants to say, Open it; but all at once it feels as if there is something else in the envelope, something my mother knows about, but I do not; and my words fail me.

So we wait. I kneel on the arm of the blue tweedy sofa in the front room and look down the length of the avenue to the corner with Coronation. When I see my father's grey gabardine and his shiny black hair and shoes I feel sick; not real sick, the kind that needs a bowl, but worry sick, that sticks like porridge in the throat.

My father opens the letter while my mother looks over his shoulder. And then he smiles at me, the new-house smile, and I know that it is all right, that there is only good news in the envelope.

You've passed, he says. You're going to Clifton Hall.

And he says Well done, well done, over and over again, all through the evening at intervals, before Z Cars, after Z Cars, before he goes down to the Ferry to tell everyone that his daughter has got in to Grammar School.

But my mother just hugs me and I am cold and hot with my heart pulsing in my throat and the Deering with its black uniform receding from my mind; gone out of my life for ever.

I am going to school in a stately home. My new school is the ancestral home of the Clifton family, an ancient red-brick house with its own church and grounds and gateposts topped with the Clifton symbol of a phoenix rising out of a crown. The phoenix is on the school crest and we will have it on our berets and blazers, as well as a uniform of purple and gold and white, purple skirts and cardigans for winter and purple and white striped frocks for summer. In May I go with

75

my mother and father for an interview with Miss Heron, the headmistress. Miss Heron smiles at me and shakes my hand, and says she knows that I will do very well. She is tall with wispy red hair and thin pencilled eyebrows and she wears her long black gown at all times, sweeping in and out of classrooms and bearing down on girls rushing between the old and new buildings to ask about their choice of 'O' level' subjects. As I will learn, she also knows, and will always know, every girl in the school by name.

Every girl, because this is a girls' school. I have won my way into a world I only know from books: the world of Enid Blyton's Malory Towers, a school of turrets and castellations and the dramas of best friends; a defensible place, where to be good and do well will be a shield against the world outside. At night my mother hangs my new summer frock on a hanger from the picture rail in my room and instead of looking at the blue and black horses on my wallpaper as I fall asleep I watch the dress.


Christmas. The world feels steady once again; my purple and gold uniform hangs in the wardrobe and there are frost flowers on my bedroom windows; beautiful flowers, cold as stars, obscuring the outside. It is Christmas Eve, and at the bottom of my bed, hanging over the footboard, is a white pillowcase. In a couple of hours my mother and father will creep in, very quietly, with presents in their hands, and out of respect I will close my eyes while they pack the nylon sack with rustling boxes. Sometimes I have fallen asleep by the time they come, so that when I wake up and see the square shapes filling up the pillowcase it is as if there really was a Santa Claus, and although I have known since I was eight years old that he does not exist there is a pleasure in the residue of him, a comfort in the secret that is not really kept from me.

Tonight, though, I stay awake a long time. The taxi that will bring my grandparents for the festive season is late. I try to stay awake but I doze a little, so that when I wake in the night I realize the taxi must have come while I was asleep, because through my bedroom wall I can hear my grandfather playing the piano on the landing. He is playing his favourite piece, the Moonlight Sonata. It is not Chopin, like most of the music my mother plays, but it feels the same: slow, soft-pedalled, gentle. My grandfather's fingers come down slowly on the notes, staying on each sound until the echo moves it into the next. The Moonlight Sonata is easy to remember, he says, because it is all groups of three notes. The first group is three liquid notes climbing up the scale, *do, do, do*. The second group has an urgency about it: it is the same note played three times, a higher note with a long and a short and a long, loud-pedal note, *daa*-da-*daa*. I listen and I start to fall asleep again and I dream that my grandfather bends sideways and smiles at me from behind his dark glasses and says, Do you hear that change in the music? and I nod. And he says, That's Beethoven trying to reach the nineteenth century.

And does he? I say. But then I jump awake because the tune has gone suddenly wrong. My grandfather has stumbled over the keys so that they clash together, black notes falling into white, left and right hands losing their sense of one another; and then there is a hiatus, a blank minute before the music resumes, dipping invisibly from the loud pedal to the soft, slipping back into quietness as the movement comes to its end.

I call out.

Grandpa?

There is a pause and then the sound of my mother's voice:

I thought you were asleep.

Where's Grandpa, I say.

Another pause and then she says,

Grandpa's not very well. He's had to go to hospital.

I sit up. The bedroom door is ajar, to let a slice of comforting light into the room, but my mother does not come in.

Will he be here for Christmas Day? I say.

I hear the creak of the piano-stool as my mother gets up, the soft thud of the piano-lid shuttering the keys.

Of course he will, she says. Why don't you say a prayer for him to get well quickly and go back to sleep.

I say the prayer. But I no longer know who to direct it to.

Perhaps that is why on Christmas day itself, the day that nothing can be allowed to spoil, he does not come; but we smile and exchange gifts as if we are happy; while my grandfather fades quietly away behind a curtain in the General Hospital, my grandmother and my mother coming and going throughout the day, taking turn and turn about between keeping Christmas and keeping vigil until it is all over.

They tell me when I wake on Boxing Day.


Afterwards, when the winter of 1966 has become the summer of peace and love, I begin to miss my grandfather. I miss the gentle man who showed me fossils in a drystone wall, I miss the dark brown glasses and white cotton jacket that he always wore, I miss the smell of the Navy Cut lodged like a pen in his hand. I miss Beethoven, straining with his deaf ears towards the nineteenth century. But the most persistent image is a memory of my grandfather that is not mine, just a story I have been told. It is an image from the war, of my mother and my grandfather in tin hats, walking through Wilford together in the blackout, fire-watching as invisible planes strafe the power station. Planes spilling streams of lightspots in the sky that twinkle and then go out; leaving just an after-image on the eyelids, like the sparks from the trains that do not run any more.

## 7

## *Elvira*

It is 1967, a year after my grandfather's death, and I am singing *White Christmas*. I am singing it not in my back garden but on a makeshift stage, leaning against an upright piano played by someone I have never met. I am wearing a long dress with puff sleeves and a full skirt made up of layers of pale pink net, but my voice is high and nervous. There is a hot light on my face, blotting out the faces of the people in the three rows of chairs in front of me. I hardly sing any more, since the disused swing was taken down in the garden; but, suddenly, on this stage at a children's drama club, I realize how I miss it. There is a place for sadness here, a place where it can fly, be made beautiful again.

It is a strange theatre, this basement of a rundown house in a part of the city scheduled for early demolition; the largest of a labyrinth of cellars, with a low ceiling and swirls of thick plaster on the walls like dirty icing, resembling the polystyrene caverns of a *Star Trek* planet. The cellar is lit by pink bulbs strung along the walls and the children around me, each waiting his or her turn at performance, are transformed by costume, fairies, angels, outlaws; swords and wands and black cloaks with constellations on them, ballet tutus and cardboard crowns. I have brought my own costume from home, although it is not quite my own, in the way of the Red Queen costume which was made for me – it is a dress my mother wore, in a long-ago village entertainment, perhaps in the war. Pinned and tucked at the back, the alterations out of sight until I grow.

I take a breath, ready for the last verse of my performance. I wonder if the music sounds joyful to the audience, full of the happiness of Christmas, or – the reason I chose the song – full of the sadness of it. Their faces are in shadow; I cannot tell what they are feeling, what emotions they might be hiding in the dark. They see me, when I can not see them. The experience is new, and strangely familiar.

As I finish there is a moment of fear before the audience claps. There are no oohs and aahs for me, but a reasonable level of applause. I bow and move slowly towards the back of the stage, unable to see where I am going.

The drama club does not last very long. When I return after the summer holidays the house is gone; the railings at the front are twisted and behind them the scoured sandy earth smokes with the dust of recent demolition. But the pull of performance remains. I have become used to seeing my mother up on the stage in Wilford's drama group, married to strange men with dark greasepaint circles round their eyes; as a child, when her onstage husband ill-treats her, I cry for her distress, and a woman in the audience turns round to me and says, It's not real, duckie.

But I have learned that they are real, these emotions that we do not show at home. I know they are stored up, and kept for use in the other life of performance. These lives, or the outer skins of them, are stored in the wardrobe in the spare bedroom of no. 26, a room theoretically kept in readiness for grandparents to stay, whenever they should need to. There is a double bed with a pale blue shiny bedspread, a kidney-shaped dressing table with a skirt, and a large oak wardrobe with carving on its doors like the pews in church. It is a cold room for sleeping, being built over the garage; on winter mornings the bedspread feels slippery, and a silvery mist films the furniture and leaves dark fingerprints. But the room has another function. The oak wardrobe is full of costumes: costumes for drama group productions, costumes for village fêtes, for school plays, almost all of them run up or altered on my mother's Singer sewing machine. There is a stiff white net with satin bodice, worn for my appearance at age five as the May Queen at the Rectory Garden Party, and a coronet strung with seed-pearls as a crown; and there is my Red Queen costume, the dress decorated with red felt hearts and the stiff peaked headdress only slightly yellowed, the musty smell of anger hanging around it.

There are ladies' clothes, too, long satin skirts and ruffled blouses and hats with bows and ostrich feathers for the drama group's period productions, clothes which my friends and I have occasionally borrowed for dressing up, but which still do not fit me. It is a matter of waiting, a strange inbetween time when shoes slur round on feet and boys lose their voices. Since my musical performance I too feel as if I am losing my voice, or stretching for notes that are lower down the scale, so that the sounds I make can echo the visible changes I see in the mirror. And what I covet, as I become in 1967 'one of those teenagers,' is a different kind of voice. It is understood that, now that I am old enough, I may be inaugurated into the Wilford Players. First affiliated to the Women's Institute, and later to the British Legion, the drama group is first and last my mother's creation, a Thursday night escape from home in a chilly underheated village hall of acting and production and set design. The plays put on twice a year are not high drama but parochial and domestic, three-acters by Falkland Carey and Wilfred Massey that exist, as Wilford does at that time, in a kind of Ealing England of certainties and happy endings. Plays whose titles tell what kind of entertainment is on offer: *Toad in the Hole, The Bride and the Bachelor, No Time for Fig-Leaves.* In the programmes it's possible to identify patterns in the roles: the alternation of the male lead between genial Eric and tall, sensitive Ken; mothers and spinsters shared out between Sheila and Barbara; and now, the younger sister of the family played by Roberta Plumb, in the shortest of miniskirts; too young for the romantic leads, for negligées and clinches, endlessly cast in the role of the bride's little sister.

In 1967 the play is *The Bride and the Bachelor*, a comedy about a ghost father who returns from the grave to chivvy his reluctant daughter Serena into marriage. When the play opens, the bride's sister Barbara is reading *From Here to Eternity* over the phone to a girlfriend, while her sister dithers over whether to marry handsome American Joe Tilney. Serena is, the play makes clear, a beauty; the sister merely clever, but, worse than that, too young to be taken for the bride. In every scene, Serena is centre stage, her hair smooth and coiffured: she poses first in a pale blue baby-doll nightdress, then in her wedding dress. Barbara is mostly off at stage left or right, half-hidden by the sofa, lost at the back of the stage: sometimes showing a knee beneath a skirt of pink chiffon, a shoulder, a tress of long lank hair beside an upturned face, battling for inclusion. Barbara has more lines than her sister, but her only weapons are her outdated schoolgirl dialect (*I say, Jennifer*) and her encyclopaedic knowledge. She loses every time to seniority. Sex is still a risqué novel, not a possibility.

But in the scheme of things, in this world of happy endings, Barbara will grow up and get her man. She has only to play enough younger sisters and eventually the clinch with Joe Tilney will come to her. For now, trapped in the Barbara-who-is-not-me, I dream of the day when I will acquire Serena's wardrobe and romantic status, but I do not only dream; I plan and scheme romances beyond the play, that take place not on the stage but at the drama party after the play which is held at the house of the producer, in this case my own house.

My plans do not include my glasses.

During my years at Wilford School my hereditary and progressive short-sightedness has escaped detection. As I grow older, I have to creep more often from my place to read the blurry fractions of the sums on the board, but at Clifton Hall even the front row of desks is no longer close enough. My mother takes me to an elderly optician who tells me that if I do not wear my glasses all day long my sight will become worse and worse; he issues me a pair of spectacles identical to my mother's, black plastic frames winged at the outside corners, with thick glass lenses that shrink the eyes behind them.

On the bus I feel the glasses pinch my nose, I feel the hard black pressure on the bone behind each ear, as if my head was held straight between pincers. I know that Joe wears glasses to read his lines, but that for men this does not matter. The two lines of the cruellest verse in the world recite themselves in my aching ears all the way home.

But there is one place where even my mother must find her way half-blind around the furniture. Spectacles reflect the spotlights, and as such are not allowed on stage. I extend this prohibition easily to the after-play party, leaving the greasepaint applied for the performance on my face: blue in the sockets of my eyes, brown underneath, a line extending almost to my temples. My eyes shine back at me from the hand-mirror, big enough at last to balance out my eyebrows. The self I see there fills me with excitement.

Downstairs my mother is pouring out the drinks. She is happy, because the play has gone well. Pleased to have the house full of friends who will stay long after my father has made his excuses and gone to bed.

What would Barbara like, she says, and I nominate a gin and orange, which I have chosen because of the sweetness of the orange and the wonderful, throat-catching smell of the clear strong spirit that floats on its stickiness, that sends the first swallow to the back of the head.

She looks at me for a moment. Then she says Well, why not, and pours the drink. I gulp it till my eyes water and wait for Joe.

Joe is late, and he does not come alone. He has brought a girlfriend with him, a blonde in a trendy dress of psychedelic whirls, her hair piled in platinum rolls and ringlets on top of her head, tough hair that shines like the hair of a Sindy doll, like the strawy wigs on the mannequins in Griffin's window. Her makeup gleams too, as if it is not quite dry, as if there is foundation on her cheeks but no powder to take away the shine. She sits on Joe's knee, and the psychedelic dress splits into a V around her crossed bare legs. While Joe introduces her I stand back, clutching my sticky drink.

I go out into the hall. In the mirror my face looks orange, my skin feels dry and taut with the loose powder blotted thickly on my cheeks with my mother's swansdown puff. My eyelids are poster-painted turquoise blue, blank blue eyes above my real hazel ones. I raise my eyebrows and my scalp moves stiffly underneath my fringe, wrinkling my forehead into waves that set like cracks in plaster. I feel the hot light and the stagnant air of the children's theatre.

I take a step backward, until the face in the mirror blurs.

There was never anything very contemporary in the Wilford Players' productions, but shortly after *The Bride and the Bachelor* the group seems to drift further into costume drama, performing plays with fairytale and medieval settings that make full use of my mother's facility for dressmaking. One such play, a sequel to Sleeping Beauty, moves the adjudicator of the local Drama Festival to applaud the efforts of the wardrobe mistress but – if he may say so - to mourn the absence at the Festival of 'real plays' dealing with the human dilemma.

He is right, of course. It is 1969, and more ambitious groups are tackling the unflinching work of Osborne and Orton and Pinter. But what the adjudicator does not see is the larger time-warp which does not just enclose Barbara and Joe but informs the whole ethos of the Players, an ethos which seems to proceed straight from my mother. For her, the drama of the 60s is not a brave new world of honesty; the Wilford Players' gentle costumed world is part of an ongoing repair for an earlier time when things went wrong.

In the darkest days of the war, while the grey crosses of Spitfires and Hurricanes do battle with the black crosses of Messeschmitts in the sky, and women with their hair in turbans scuttle through the streets below, Noël Coward writes the play *Blithe Spirit*. He writes it during a week's stay in the Fountain Suite at Portmeirion in North Wales, a fantasy village of Italianate buildings and piazzas looking out over a

Welsh bay, while in the cities the women in turbans wait for telegrams with bad news about husbands, sons, lovers; bad news which, if they are true to Coward's world, they will receive with stoicism and impenetrable dignity. These qualities permeate the prose of the plays, prose that is elegant and polished and clipped; almost literally so, leaving a sense that at the end of his characters' pithy speeches Coward has broken off, left the messy, inelegant and often incoherent business of real emotion in his head. But in 1941, as the audience for the first night of *Blithe Spirit* makes its way around the black yawn of a bomb crater to reach the door of the theatre, Coward's prose is something solid, a reassurance that they too will hold together, that their voices will be steady and word-perfect in time of need. From that time onwards – my mother is sixteen in 1941 - and even by the late sixties, her devotion to Noël and all his works is the devotion of a woman who will behave impeccably though the sky should fall down on her head.

And – though I do not yet know this - it will, and has.

It is my mother's idea that to celebrate the Master's 70th birthday in 1969, the Wilford Players should put on a production of *Blithe Spirit*. At the initial readings of the play, there is never any question but that my mother will play Elvira, Charles Condomine's first wife, recalled from the dead during the séance organized as research for a book her former husband is writing. Something in the low pitch and softness of my mother's voice suits the ghostly seductress, her voice dipping to an octave I have never heard her play on the piano. She plays her voice as she would play Chopin or Schubert with her hands, with calm control, fitting herself to the lines with ease, trusting them, allowing them to speak a part of her that I have never seen, that predates my existence.

For Elvira, the mischievous ghost-wife of the play, is not like the purse-lipped women Coward left behind in forties London. She is dead, and her death releases her from the wartime straitjacket of good behaviour. Elvira breaks things, mocks Charles' second, and much duller, wife and seduces him, protected by the cloak of invisibility that leaves her visible only to her husband and the audience. She is a sensual being, at ease with her body and free of it, draping herself over mantelpieces, over sofas, over Charles himself, boneless and fluid in her fluid garments. Like Ariel, after whom the play is named, she comes and goes when she pleases.

For once, perhaps for the first time in my life, it will be my place to stand behind my mother. There is no part for me in the play, or at least not one that is offered, not even the small part of the *savant* Edith, the screaming maid who senses the presence of the spirit. I know I will not get this part, because my teenager's voice is formless and frightened but still obedient: I am not yet ready for screaming, for releasing the voice that will allow me to break out of other people's words. As the decade of freedom draws to its close I will sit far back in the audience, my glasses placed firmly on my nose, my gaze fixed on my mother.

There is one photograph of my mother as Elvira, wearing the costume she designed and made herself, running up yard after yard of hemming on the Singer, its treadle rocking constantly through the dark December evenings of 1969. She is posing not on the stage but in our dining room at home, a pale figure standing in front of dark blue curtains. The costume is full-length, with an underdress of olive crêpe and an overdress, or negligée, of silver-grey. Her head is turned to one side, her dark hair covered by an ash-blond wig, her eyelids tinted silver, her skin the emptied colour of shock, or faintness, or death. Through the folds of olive crêpe her knee is slightly lifted, as if she is about to walk out of the photograph, but her eyes look back into the corner of the room, towards the fire, the sewing-box, the paper Christmas garland hanging limp from the picture-rail. They are huge eyes, red-tinted with the flash, a wistfulness in them that has nothing to do with farce. It is to do with where Elvira will go at the end of the play, where Ariel goes. A kind of afterthought, projected forward into the cold space of the room.

And there is another thought, one projected back. Seeing something in the room that the photographer cannot see.

*Blithe Spirit* is my mother's finest hour. A local drama critic, who generally spares a line or two for the Wilford Players in his newspaper reviews, on this occasion fills a long slim column with his comments on the production. He calls my mother's performance 'positively brilliant,' 'flawless'; it is the 'gem of the evening.' For a month or two, she has her leg pulled by family and friends about 'H.J.', her courtly admirer. She smiles, and pastes the write-up into her Wilford Players scrapbook; a remnant of the olive crêpe is made into an evening bag for the next production, hand-stitched and trimmed with pearly sequins shaped like flowers; hand-stitching that makes no sound, that continues long into the night.

One evening, during the production of Blithe Spirit, before I have gone to bed, my mother takes the bag from her sewing box, and something white is pulled out with it: a scarf, made of thin white fabric about a yard square, hand-hemmed with puckered edges where the stitches have pulled the cloth. The scarf is not plain but printed front and back with maps, maps of places my mother has never been to, and never will. The maps are in colour, the place-names in tiny writing readable only by bringing the scarf close to the face. There are stains on the scarf, paint perhaps, salmon-pink, charcoal grey, crimson. On one side the maps are of Brittany, Normandy, Belgium, Holland, the Pyrenees; on the other the south of France and Spain, with an inset down one side of the Swiss-German borderlands, the border itself a thick crimson line curving and looping across the silk. Frontiers – the word appears in each legend accompanying the maps – are all crimson. This relic is of the wartime years of *Blithe Spirit*; only it is not of Elvira's world but that of the women in their turbans; the world of another play, a play called *Still Life*; a woman's role Coward wrote before Elvira, a woman from the world he ran from to the peace and quiet of North Wales.

I ask. Who did the scarf belong to, I say.

My mother removes the thimble from her finger, takes the scarf gently into her hands, and starts to refold it; staring, speaking into space.

We were engaged, in the war, she says. But he died. His name was John.

I don't know why I leave it there.

By four o'clock the next day Granny Bailey has arrived at no.26, ready to take up temporary residence for the festive season in the spare room. She goes early to bed, complaining of indigestion. By eleven my mother is on the green telephone in the hall, calling the emergency doctor. My grandmother has *passed malina stools*, the doctor says, reporting her condition to the hospital. She will be admitted straight away. She is carried gently down to the ambulance, moaning softly, the belt from her new quilted housecoat trailing after her down the stairs.

As long as my grandmother is ill, my mother will put her life away as if it were separable from her. The scarf is hidden, out of sight again. The play is done. The curtains close.

## 8

## *Dead Letters*

I am lying in my mother's bed, watching myself in the great Gothic mirror on top of the dressing table that stands at the end of the bed, its glass arched like a church window into a prayer-peak. My head is tilted to one side, my cheek hugging my shoulder; the top half of my body is propped stiffly on raised pillows. The rust-coloured expanse of the brocade bedspread has been pulled up to my armpits, but my arms and hands are out of sight. My neck is hot and pulsing, but I cannot see the pulse for the thick white bandage wound around my neck.

The bandage has a familiar smell. It smells of kaolin, the pink medicine that is the family remedy for nausea. I try to straighten my head, but my neck is set in its position. I slip my right hand slowly from the bedclothes and feel the bandage. The lint is hardening and drying like plaster; like the plaster that was wrapped around my wrists after I fell from my riding-school pony onto a frozen field. The hard white arm that I carried with me to school, that was scribbled over with every name but mine.

I call for my mother. *Mum*. The word sounds strange, half in my mouth, half in my throat. I try to shout, and hear her coming up the stairs.

It is not that I do not remember becoming ill. I remember a Christmas Eve of playing cards and eating salted peanuts and drinking Babycham, and being sick. I remember waking up on Christmas Day to find my head bent over to my right, my neck fixed and sore, a tracery of little lumps, like hidden beads beneath my skin, running down from my right ear to my shoulder, my voice muffled and hard to understand, like the voice of my deaf cousin. I remember Dr Clarke coming, prescribing a hot clay poultice for my neck, poultices my mother must apply twice a day.

It is that I do not know what is wrong with me.

My mother comes into the room and straightens my pillows. Her bedjacket and nightie are on my father's bed, and my father has moved temporarily into the spare room, so that she can look after me at night. It is the first time we have slept in the same room since I was small, but we are not uncomfortable together. On the contrary, we are comfortable, mutually absorbed in the business of caring, in the removal of the poultices, the gentle washing of my neck with a warm soapy flannel, the making of a new pad from old handkerchiefs wrapped around cotton wool soaked in the milky clay liquid, the unwinding and rewinding of the bandages. When the poultices are off I scratch my neck, very carefully; the bumps and hollows of my neck are smooth, but there are stray traces of dried clay sticking to my skin, tiny hard ridges like the grey lunar landscapes I have seen on the television. There is no television upstairs, no unfolding Apollo future to watch, but there are books. In the evenings my mother reads to me from *Pickwick Papers*, leaving out the misery of Pickwick in the debtors' prison, and concentrating instead on the passages of farce and the comic characters of Sam Weller and Mr Jingle. Like Sam, who substitutes w for v in his speech, and vice versa, I have found that when I try to speak I cannot say my letters properly. Whole consonants are lost to me: *r, k, g, v,* the *th* in *then.* On the days when I feel well enough to paint, I write the missing letters in watercolour round the rim of my china mixing plate. They make a hard word, a word that is beyond my present power of speech. Because I am unable to open my mouth fully, my mother makes me tiny square sandwiches that I chew laboriously with my front teeth. Muffled by gums, in the narrowed opening of my mouth, my adult molars, unbrushed, begin slowly to decay. I lean back, quiet, on my pillows, listening to the transpositions of Sam and the stuttered sentences of Alfred Jingle. And, when my mother leaves the room, withdrawing into the romances in my head, sealed off from the world.

Two weeks after I fall ill, Dr Clarke visits again, and writes out a new prescription. My new white medicine smells sweet, it froths in the spoon like yeast. After the very first dose I wake in the morning with my neck unlocked, my head moving, slowly, back to the perpendicular.

The medicine working this miracle is penicillin.

On the second night I turn my head gently, experimentally, as I swallow the four teaspoons of my dose. I imagine the liquid surging down my neck like a smooth white river, melting away the stinging clusters of dark bacteria in its path, lubricating my vocal chords so I can use my voice again.

I have lost a third of my weight, and been away from school six weeks. The world I return to will be bright and hard and loud. And I am fearful of how it may have shifted in my absence. When I walk back through the gates of Clifton Hall in March, I feel as if it is the voices of the other girls, rather than my own, that have changed.

I am weak and nervous going back. My voice is still lacking consonants, and the cuffs of my white blouse gap around my wrists. My uniform feels stiff and borrowed, like the clothes my mother still sends out to displaced persons in East Germany. I make my way up the stairs in the new building to the first floor, and walk through an empty classroom to the short flight of stairs leading to the Biology lab. Through the closed double doors I can hear the girls of Four Alpha laughing and shouting across the room to one another. And I can smell the smell of formaldehyde. On the windowsills around the lab that is this year's form room there are glass cases full of dead things, most of which I cannot identify, objects that look like swollen mushrooms and marrow-bones and potatoes; and one that I can, a tiny mouse, a bleached shade of beige like all the other objects, curled up in the liquid with his eyes closed. The only specimens in the laboratory that are not dead are the locusts, warmed in their glass case by a stump of a lightbulb that is permanently on, a crawling mass of them clinging to a starved stem of some sort of plant. The locusts too are beige. Most of the time they play as dead as their laboratory companions, but occasionally they move, crawling like a mass of bees or ants, responding to taps or bangs on their warm sheet of glass. A few locusts do not join the mass but look outward from the glass with mournful pinhead eyes.

The smell catches on one of the remaining lumps in my throat. I start to cough and the double doors open. A girl emerges and pelts down the steps, stopping when she sees me.

Oh, she says, Mrs Williams said you were back today.

I try to smile and say yes, and hello, two words that I can manage in full. She asks me how I am, but I see other words gathering in her head, a flush of waiting in her face that is not benign.

What about Davy Jones, then, she says, and I say, What about him?

She hears the change in my voice. She looks at me, she takes me in.

Haven't you heard, she says, pushing the door into the lab, that he got married in secret over a year ago, it's been in all the papers for days?

I look into the lab. The girls of Four Alpha are sitting either side of the room, on the fixed benches that run around the lab, swinging their legs. They do not stop talking as I enter, they carry on, but they look at me. No, I want to say, I haven't seen a paper for weeks, I haven't even watched the news. The words rush up my throat, come to a halt at my neck.

Yes, I say. I know all about it.

Two other girls slither down from the bench and meet me just beyond the door. One of them has protruberant blue eyes, eyes that look more closely than is polite. Her lashes are long and curved, coated with flakes of mascara that spots her cheeks like black dandruff.

You've lost a lot of weight, she says. What was wrong with you?

I do not want to talk, not to these girls with their unblinking eyes. It is taking all my energy to keep my face still.

It was my neck, I say. A sort of glandular fever.

They take a step backwards.

Glandular fever's catching, she says. They shouldn't have let you come back.

I shake my head. Dr Clarke has assured me that I am not infectious.

They whisper and move off to their benches, banging on the locusts' glass case as they sweep by. For minutes afterwards the girls continue to laugh and to repeat to one another, over and over, *lanular feer, lanular feer*.

I reach the bench where my best friend Karin is sitting. She has had her fine hair permed, and she is wearing a shoelace bracelet that I do not remember, but she has placed her bag on my stool the way she has always done when I am late.

I was going to tell you, she says quietly.

On the bench there is a copy of *16* magazine with a marker in it. When I open the magazine the banner headline runs across two pages: *Davy: You Should Have told Us!* above a picture of the happy family: Linda, the smiling wife with smooth dark hair, and Davy, holding a baby in a blue smock. The story underneath the picture is blunt about the reasons for Davy's secret marriage. After eighteen months of teen adoration, the Monkees' star is in decline. Newer, unmarried idols are stripping photos of the cute Mancunian with the Bournville eyebrows from bedroom walls: Scott Walker, Peter Frampton, David Cassidy. Davy himself has issued only the statement that he loves his fans, he hopes they'll understand.

I look at the picture. It is a good one. Davy's mouth is slightly open, his hair feathered softly around his face in the layers which are just becoming trendy, the blue shirt open around a tanned half-diamond of smooth hairless chest. If I cut away the wife who stands behind him, looking over his shoulder, I can back the photograph with cardboard and cover it with clear gummed plastic, as I have done with other favourites that I carry round with me. Only just below Davy's right ear is Linda's mouth, open in a smile that reveals a bright shield of American teeth, moulded like a spur of bone to the smooth curve of his neck. No, I do not understand, but I recognize. I recognize the silence of the lie, and the sudden sound of the truth rushing through my head like the water in an ear-syringe; finding the place in my imagination that I thought was safe, unreachable. My story has never reached words, and now it is annihilated. I strike it from my brain.

Mrs Williams calls the register. She is about to pass over my name, but when my voice answers she looks up. The girls giggle softly once again.

At the end of the lesson I tell Karin I have to go to the toilet, and she says she will wait for me. I go into the toilets with the shiny grey Formica doors and lock myself in. Since my illness I have been unable to move my bowels properly, and every morning my mother has given me a tiny sweet square of Ex-Lax. Now my muscles are contracting, but I cannot free my body of the dark compacted mass within my gut. For twenty minutes I shift from one damp leg to the other on the seat, pushing with little silent gasps until there are starry spots of blood on the white bowl. Outside, Karin is telling the other girls how ill I have been, although she has no explanation of the illness. They pass from talking of my odd deaf voice to Davy Jones, and still I cannot go. The outer toilet door squeaks on its hinges as Karin comes in looking for me.

Robbie, she says, are you still in here?

I squat shivering on the seat, sweating, exhausted. My voice has sunk so deep down into my throat even I cannot hear it. Eventually, baffled, Karin goes away.

*Cervical adenitis*, Dr Clarke has written in bold, black, and surprisingly legible words on the certificate I gave to Mrs Williams. Even if I understood the words, I could not say them.

Slowly I recover. I begin to put on weight again. A lady who walks the village in a beret and an old belted raincoat, tells my mother that what I need is glucose, and for the next two weeks I take two tablespoons a day of the fine white sweet powder. My consonants return, one by one, filling in the gaps in my words, but not my consuming devotion to Davy. I have learned something else; that reality can find out even the deepest places in the imagination, unless they are kept well hidden. I experience new passions, but they are more careful ones: I become interested in actors again, actors in a kind of theatre that is different, where the rules of the drama are not those followed in Wilford Players' productions.

In the new theatre of the late 60s the wall between viewed and viewer is not collapsed, but it is permeable. These are the days of theatre in the round, days when the audience can find itself drawn into the performance. At the brand new Nottingham Playhouse, with its self-consciously designed columns of naked concrete and black-painted steel girders, my mother and I see a production of Julius Caesar. Caesar is black, and dressed in Victorian costume; but it is the mobility of the actors, leaping on and off the stage, vaulting empty stalls and slumping wounded at the feet of the patrons in the best seats, that unnerves and excites me. There is an apparent removal of the division between actor and audience, but I am not fooled; I see how the actors are still in control, how the audience is required only to react. But I am tired of weakness and passivity. I want to be strong. Most of all, I want to take part. When one of Brutus' henchmen approaches me I draw back, but I scan the stage for someone I might approach. A young man who has a minor and non-speaking role in the production, and spends most of his onstage time leaning on a broken Grecian column at the rear of the stage, is picked out by the spotlight that highlights his blond uncovered head among the gunmetal helmets, and after the performance I study his portrait in the foyer. It is a dreamy face, the eyes a dilute blue, the indirect gaze unintimidating. I write to the young man, and he replies.

I am anxious not to make the mistake I made with Joe. I read the letter over and over again. I have received responses to fan letters before, and I know that there is a formula to the response. Thanks for the letter, a reference to the actor's next role, perhaps a small signed photograph. All these are in the young man's letter, but two things are different. He encourages me to come to the next play, a production of *Twelfth Night* with *a very pretty set.* And he says *I look forward very much to hearing from you again.* The biro has spluttered over the *I* in this sentence, but elsewhere the handwriting is straight and firm and unembellished. I take him at his words, and I write a second letter. The voice on the page is bold, confident, and it does not stumble. I tell the actor the date of the performance I will be attending. I tell him that I will be in Row C, number 18, and that I will be wearing a red jumper. And finally I tell him that I too am an actress, albeit an amateur. I invite him to the next Wilford Players' production as my guest.

The young man has warned me that his face will be masked by a false beard, so I have armed myself against failed recognition by committing his role to memory. It is a small role, one of the duke's attendants; his star still hovers in the wings, his voice is still in apprenticeship to Shakespeare's poetry. His prosaic *Will you go hunt, my lord?* cuts a flat note across Orsino's lyric longing for the fool's music; later, Curio stands aside, motionless on the stage, as the fool sings for Orsino:

> *Fly away, fly away, breath;*
> *I am slain by a fair cruel maid.*

I am looking up, straight at Curio, when I see him turn from the duke and peer out into the twilight of the audience. There is another red jumper in Row B, but its owner is watching the clown, tumbled on the apron of the stage, his voice quavering through the song. Behind the fool, Curio is elegant in doublet and hose, a rosette on his velvet hat echoed in another on his shoe; but the beard is dark, bench-brown, a rough slit cut beneath the moustache for the jut of a pink underlip. The eyes are nearly lost between hat and beard, but they see me from a distance, considering, looking down from the spotlit arbour to the half-lit stalls. I keep my gaze steady, waiting for a sign of acknowledgement, a fractional nod, the lifting of a glove. But no sign comes. Curio is frozen, his pose not new theatre but static as a medieval tableau.

I fold my damp hand round my beads, my last relic of Davy. As I turn away, a stray beam of spotlight flashes on the inside of my right lens. In my anxiety, I have forgotten the first rule of the old theatre. The young man cannot, or will not, see beyond my glasses. When his last letter comes, regretful that he is unable to accept my invitation to Wilford, the writing will be an echo of his pose: formal, stilted, in retreat.

For my appearance in the Church Hall play, to which he will not now be coming, I refuse to use the blunted sticks of communal greasepaint. This time, when I paint my face, the makeup is my own. I have bought green eyeshadow, brown liquid eyeliner, and glistening mascara with a tiny toilet-brush. These products give me back my eyes, eyes that others will see at the forthcoming school dance, though now, half-blind, I am the one scarcely able to return the compliment. People's faces, and the very edges of the world, all blur away. Within weeks, I have a boyfriend.

## *9*

## **The Dark Room**

There's a blade of north wind cutting at our faces as we cross the Toll Bridge. My father and I are walking over together, he to catch his bus into town, me to get the free school bus to Clifton Hall. My satchel is heavy, and as usual my father carries it under his arm until we part. He smiles in a way that looks as if he's setting his teeth against the wind, but the smile is real, as he strides out and overtakes the drivers in the steaming queue of cars. The days of the queue are numbered, because the weight limit on the bridge has been down to two tons for some time, and closure to traffic is already on the cards.

My father says that the cause of this is corrosion, corrosion of the part of the bridge we can't see. Beneath our feet, holding up the pebbly concrete spans and the idling cars, there's a cradle of iron, a network of thin dark struts whose metal is slowly crumbling into the river. Under the bridge a chemical equation is working itself out, an equation of the kind my father once tried to teach me on the dining room table after the tea things were cleared; a code made up of letters and numbers whose connection I could never understand: $O_2$, $H_2O$, $FE_4$. Iron plus water plus air equals iron oxide. The iron oxide is fragile and works itself loose until chunks and flecks of it crumble from the struts of the bridge, falling like red snow on the river. There are more layers of metal underneath the iron oxide, but the equation will

107

get that too until it's all gone. My father is telling the old joke about painting the Forth Bridge, but I am looking down at the river, parting itself around the cylinders driven into its bed, and thinking how strange it seems that air and water and bridges shouldn't mix. I turn, look back at the crusty red bars of the fence around the Ferry fields and imagine climbing up and sitting on the bars the way my friends and I used to; only if I jumped down now there would be flecks of iron in my underwear, on my legs.

My father stays cheerful. He will not regret the cars, but I will, though I don't know it yet. Once on the town side of the river we walk anticlockwise around the grassy roundabout, usually parting where Queen's Drive goes off to the right, and I take my satchel onto my shoulder, and wave goodbye to my father as he rushes for Wilford Road and the number 40.

Today, though, we separate at the foot of the Toll Bridge, and I walk the semicircle to Queen's Drive on my own, whipping my glasses from my face as soon as I have seen my father wave. On the curve of the roundabout before Queen's Drive is a woodyard, and a set of railings where the workmen sit and smoke before work starts for the day. The workmen stare as I pass, the way builders do, and call after me. Not *Speccy four-eyes*, like the Deering boys, but *Nice eyes*. I like the change, although I can't return the compliment; the workmen's eyes are dark smudged spots in blurry faces. I smile and start to run. A green and white bus is coming down Queen's Drive, too far away for me to see the number.

# The Memory of Bridges

I don't quite realize it but I have entered into some kind of trade-off, eyes for eyesight, compliments for semi-blindness. I'm alone walking down the ruled length of Queen's Drive, but it is daylight, and I am used to this. At night aloneness is different. Then I lose not just the edges of things, but of their centres. It is as if there is a watercolour wash over a drawing of the world, making the outlines of people and objects bleed into a dark speckled fog. At night, I have begun not to recognize things, not to recognize people. With boyfriends I have a strategy, and the strategy is to arrive at the agreed place of meeting – usually one of the scowling stone lions in the city's Market Square – a half-hour early. Sometimes, still trying for the initiative, I get it wrong, and lurch towards a tall blond Afro in a fringed suede jacket in the conviction that it is Andy, or Mick, or Trevor; more often it is safer and less embarrassing to wait, gazing into space, until my date arrives. I plead that my mind is somewhere else when finally grabbed by the elbow, when the face is close enough for me to pick out eyebrows, curls, a Zapata moustache. And yet I stick to my guns. My glasses stay unmentioned, out of sight.

While the date lasts, there is relief from the aloneness. To be with someone who will find seats in the pub, catch the barman's eye, find the right money. But at the end of every evening there is still the bridge to cross. In 1971 most boys do not have cars, and to get home from a date late at night means to queue in the Market Square for a taxi, sometimes for an hour, sometimes two. The accepted way of passing the time in the queue is snogging, but I am always raising my head, always

109

coming up for air. I do not feel safe in the dark, clinging to the lapels of my boyfriend's sheepskin and being jostled by occasionally violent drunks. For the first time I wish my father had a car like other fathers, so that I could go running from the streetlamp-lit trail of spilt beer and sick to familiar headlamps and the friendly toot of a horn; I wish I could settle back onto clean seats and be brought home, instead of looking out through the muddied glass of taxi windows, the dark back of a strange driver blocking my view of the road as I search blindly for the fare.

One night it seems there is a choice. My current boyfriend and I have left the disco early, and the last bus for the Toll Bridge has not yet left the square. I cannot see the number on the bus, but only the 47 stops outside Farmers clothes store, and after one look at the dark shadow of the queue splashed out across the square I turn to my date and say a hurried goodnight. My heart thumps as the bus goes slowly through the Meadows down Wilford Road, dropping off the few passengers as it goes.

The windows of the Cremorne Hotel at the terminus are dark and the door is bolted. I jump from the bus and run towards the end of Queen's Drive. The bus moves partway round the roundabout with me, before turning off along the embankment road on the north side of the river to go back to the garage. I cross behind it, and start up the Toll Bridge.

Somewhere in my mind there is a voice telling me that I have put myself at risk; but there is another voice, telling me that if I keep my head down, if I do not

110

look, it will somehow be all right. But as I pass the shuttered toll-house I cannot help glancing quickly up the cobbled road towards the dark squat pillars of the bridge. There is no one in sight. I pass the brick pillars emblazoned with the Clifton crest, the coronet shining orange in the streetlights. *Tenez le droit*, the motto says. Perversely I hug the lefthand side of the bridge, keeping close to the thick pipe which screens me from the black drop into the river. On the spans above the water the air changes: it is not so much damp as sharp, peppered with cold, tiny specks of water thrown up by the sporadic slap of the river against the iron cylinders in its bed. When I put my hands against my cheeks I don't feel water, just a roughness on my skin as if the iron flecks are drifting through the air and settling like red freckles on my face. The road dips down from the bridge between the Ferry Fields and I start to trot briskly, moving out from the pavement and the fenced-off sodden grass onto the deserted road.

There is a bobbing shape in the fog in front of me. Someone is on the other side of the road, walking up towards the bridge.

I have my head down again. The shape is resolving from a blob into other shapes, growing legs and arms with lighter spaces in between them. It has a voice, and the voice is male. And the voice is settling into words, words I want to keep a blur like the dark man with his arms and legs.

I look up quickly, quick as I can, no longer than a shutter-click. I see a blur of shadowed face about a yard away. The dark arm has a lighter hand sprouting from it, a hand pointing in my direction. The voice speaks again. The end of the sentence lifts up, curling into a question mark.

The words are staying as a blur. I hear them and try to keep the sounds apart so that they can't join themselves into sense. And then I flinch off to my left and run. The turn for Coronation Avenue is about fifty yards away. Above the dark line of the floodbank I can see the tops of the trees and the peaked roofs of the houses. I run full-tilt without looking back, without listening, without anything but praying that he will not follow me.

He does not follow me. But his voice does, calling something that might be reassuring, maybe not.

I pelt the length of Coronation but by the time I turn into Vernon, and see the thin light column in our front door shining down the avenue, I am walking again.

My mother opens the door to me. My father will have gone to bed some time ago, but she is waiting up with the lights blazing and the new central heating still going full-blast. She looks beyond me, out into the road. Didn't you get a taxi? she says. And I say, or I think I say, No, the last bus was just going, I walked over the bridge. My mother takes this information calmly. I don't tell her about the man, she doesn't tell me that I must never, never take that risk again. We seem to collude in unspokenness, just as I have colluded in my own half-blindness. As I take my glasses from her, the world sharpens into clarity, and I sit down in my child's chair while she makes me tea and watch the late film on the television. It is a Doris Day film, shot under bright lights with the heroine in a tight white frock and an assortment of negligées. Rock Hudson is the leading man, who looks a bit like my father, a comforting man in a suit, a man with a comforting name. Doris and Rock share a phone line, so that most of their dialogue is conducted across a split screen, and the negligées are acceptable to the 1950s censor because Rock never sees her in them. Doris is being deceived by Rock, but it will all come right in the end; the bar down the centre of the screen will melt away and be replaced by marriage and conventional happiness.

My hands are warm around my teacup as the credits roll. My mother and I go up to bed together, parting at my bedroom door. In her room my father is snoring with his mouth gaped dentist-wide. I can't see him, but I hear the sound. *Kha, kha.*

Night night then, my mother says. Sleep tight.

I lie down with my head propped on my arm, the way I did when I was small, but I do not sleep tight. In the small hours I wake with my hands against my cheeks, feeling for the iron freckles. I put on my bedside lamp and look in the mirror, stretching and prodding my skin as if I am looking for a disease. I can't see the freckles, my mother didn't see them. I lie down again and dream of scarlet fever. But it's my mother who has it, not me; she is lying there with the rash all down her throat, and I am standing at her half-open bedroom door, not daring to go in because I don't know how to make her better. She seems to be ill a long time ago, years before my frothy white medicine which would have cured her.

113

In the morning the sun is shining through the curtains. But school is nearly out and the walks with my father, like the days of the traffic, are numbered.

As the summer of 1972 draws nearer, I am doing well in all my 'O' level subjects, with the exception of Latin. I am never happier than at exam time, learning my revision notes as I learn my lines for the drama, and delivering them on cue. I have a good memory, and a cast of thought that is often called original but I know in my heart is just reaction: reaction against any kind of received wisdom, against the truth of others. Bold as a lion on paper, I embrace contrary arguments in a way which relieves the boredom of examiners and earns me extra marks. This strategy works well in English, but is of little use in Latin, which I fail spectacularly at O level with a Grade 9.

Miss Heron cannot quite understand my indifference to my failure. In all other subjects I appear the keen pupil I have always been; in Latin class alone I seem to have granted myself a licence to misbehave. My friend and I have spent every lesson ducked down behind our bags, discussing boys and ignoring the teacher's weary appeals for attention, while our chance to understand the language of the elite, the mysterious code of lawyers, doctors and *cervical adenitis* has passed us by. *A shame*, Miss Heron writes next to the grade on my 5th year report, the last one that will carry the blue swirls of her gold-nibbed Parker. At the foot of the paper, in her capacity as headmistress, she adds the enigmatic comment *Roberta must learn to look ahead*; a comment that leaves me, temporarily, also mystified.

But by the sixth form Miss Heron is gone, and I have seen the reason for her insistence on Latin. Without a Latin O level I cannot take single honours English at university, and have to opt instead for a joint Art History and English combination, a course for which there are fewer places and greater competition. I am interviewed by my home university, misdiagnose a late Leonardo, and am summarily rejected. It is now Art College or nothing – since employment, for a Clifton Hall girl with A levels, is considered to be pretty well synonymous with nothing.

My father, who has worked all his life, does not disagree with this. He has said little about my academic lowering of sights. All through my schooldays he has stood by the side of my learning, hearing my times tables and the capital cities of the world, leaving Arthur Jepson hanging on another line while I recite my A level results over the phone. But as my life stutters he retreats, he steps aside from the work of recovery which is my mother's unspoken domain. And, once I am enrolled at Art College, there is no more homework or equations for him to help me with. I too now take the number 40 bus into town, but a full hour later than my father. The unstructured hours of college leave me still in bed, while my father crosses the bridge alone, without my satchel and the cars.

You know, says the tutor, squinting at my life drawing of the bodybuilder, The college often does some weeding out at Christmas. This isn't really up to scratch.

I look down at my pencil sketch, which has a hard black outline around it as all my drawings do. We have been given A1 sheets of cartridge paper for the exercise, and my paper keeps slipping from the board onto the floor. My drawing is not especially small, but on this steppe of paper my man looks lost, his arms held out like sausages clear of his sides. He is a moon-man without a space suit, an Antarctic explorer in the white flat of an ice-field. It's only in the outline you can really see him, and the outline is one of the things that the tutor does not like. The other students fill their A1 sheets with charcoal scribbles of concentric circles that build up into thigh and bicep and buttock, somehow drawing from the inside out. But I start with my outline. I don't know how to do anything else.

The bodybuilder's is the first body I have really been called on to observe. He seems all body, the muscles of his chest and shoulders like eggs bulging under a tight chocolate skin, a small static head in profile, like a coin, above them. In my drawings bodies usually stop at mid-chest, and if the drawing is to be full-length, as it is when I am sketching happy couples of the kind to be found on Gordon Fraser greeting cards, then I clothe the girl in a flowing dress which curves in swirls and folds around the bottom of the paper, covering torso and legs and, in general, the torso and legs of her boyfriend. But what the tutor is asking for is not a likeness that drains down from a pretty face to a delicate

116

pattern of avoidance. It is something real, in three dimensions, something I am failing to see. My drawing is flat, not really of a man but of a figure rolled out from the store of my imagination. And the bodybuilder, even if uncannily still, is solid, it is possible to walk right round him and try out different angles. But walking around him is something I never think of doing.

And if I continue to fail, I will be *weeded out*. In the two months since the end of school I have gone from best to worst in class.

It seems to me that I am the only lost soul on the course. My best friend Karin has acquired new friends, my current boyfriend flirts with every other girl on the course, the other tutors - not like the teachers at Clifton Hall, but strange beings with cropped lemon hair and a perpetual tone of sarcasm - are dismissive of my artistic projects, laughing and stubbing out their Consulates as I squint at my latest attempt at artwork.

Somebody should get you a pair of glasses, darling.

It is like school, with the uniforms burnt away. And instead of uniforms the students who will succeed take care to find a costume that defines them, the wackier the better. There are boys in green eyeshadow, girls with strange serpentine tattoos, boys in Doc Martens and Rupert trousers checked in black and primrose yellow. And the students' artwork, artfully, complements the costume. Jeremy, who owns the Rupert trousers, and will one day be famous as the musical creator of the Specials, anticipates his own future by building a giant amplifier and sitting in it.

Forget about school, says one of the tutors, looking at my collage, which is the word *Change* with the letters made up of fashion photographs from different decades. Forget everything you learned and start again.

But I don't know how to start again, not under this bright light that seems to have distilled the casual malice into its spitting fluorescence, a light that clarifies nothing but reduces the few shapes I can still recognize to whiteout.

Somebody should get me a pair of glasses. But what I want now is dark ones, like my Grandpa Bailey's, to protect my eyes from the glare.


John is that rare thing in the 1970s, a mature student. Not only mature, but married, with a beard that does not tend to the wispy but is neatly trimmed, and a perpetual outfit of beige polo-neck and brown cord jeans. The only reason he is not taken for one of the tutors is his lack of theatre. He is kind, sensible, and he has the key to the darkroom.

The rest of us are expected to pick up technical skills as we need them, but John has arrived at college with his knowledge of photography ready-made. This skill is a password to the facilities of the darkroom tucked away in the top corner of the studio, where John uses the enlarger and the white metal trays containing the various chemicals of photography. Here, where I go to hide from the tutors, I watch John hanging films out to dry, long shining spools of negatives swinging gently from their bulldog clips; I watch as sheets of blank white paper are slipped into the developer, the stop bath, the tray of fixer, as the shapes of leaves and hands and faces emerge, building into images under the red light. John takes a photograph of me where I sit cross-legged on the darkroom stool. As the negative passes through the window of the enlarger, I see my pale hair and eyes with white pinpoint pupils in a dark face projected down onto the paper.

Now for the miracle, says John.

I look down. On the blank paper floating in the white metal tray a ghostly self is appearing, a pale grey image surfacing like a half-drowned body emerging from water, returning through the polarity to positive. The paper drifts in the slosh of chemical, its greys darkening into black. I watch myself becoming solid, my eyes restored to dark. Half drowned, the liquid running from my legs.

Don't leave it in too long, says John, pushing me gently aside and flipping the print deftly into the stop bath. I see myself fixed there, held at the age of eighteen looking off to one side, a half smile on my face and an arm crooked behind my head, wearing my granddad t-shirt and the black and white striped satin maxi-skirt that hides my legs.

John is kind to me, and I will never forget it. He gives me a place to hide when hiding is all I can do. And the darkness hides me, for a while seems kinder than the light. In the soft red darkness I begin to talk again, talk that does not require any answer but brings my voice out of the liquid like my face. Talk about the new boyfriend

I have found, a different kind of boyfriend: one who listens, like John, one who does not mean me any harm. To whom, in six short days, I will be engaged.

But once outside the darkroom, under the fluorescent light, I do not wait to be weeded out. Before the spring term is over I have jumped ship and dropped out of my course, the third dimension still escaping me.

## *10*

## *Scream in Time*

Life is full of second chances, says John, and he is probably right. Except that I don't know if they are second chances. Most of the time it's echoes I'm aware of, the dull thud of something happening again, a replay of a song whose words are fixed. While at art college I have applied again, half-heartedly, to university. To my surprise, I receive an offer for the next academic year of a place at Liverpool, who seem unconcerned about my lack of Latin. The UCCA form stays unanswered on my dressing table until one morning my mother comes and sits on my bed, and asks me what I'm going to do.

Well, I don't know, I say, not now I've met Peter.

I'm sure Peter will wait for you, she says.

It's warm in bed, and my mother has brought my morning cup of tea. I lie staring at the red lining of my eyelids and think of the student flat Peter shares with a schoolfriend in the condemned slums of the Meadows, a room where the beds are mattresses on the floor covered with filthy purple sheets. I think of the ex-girlfriends, even an ex-fiance, who have accompanied Peter to college in Nottingham from their home town of Scunthorpe. But most of all I think of going far away, a feeling like the dark journey across the bridge, haloed lampposts blurring out into the distance.

My mother gets up and starts to collect the clothes I have scattered around the floor.

You're not going to take it, are you, she says, and I have a sip of hot tea and say I don't know, while she piles the clothes on the end of the bed and opens the curtains.

You should write back and tell them as soon as possible, she says, so they can offer the place to someone else.

I open my eyes and watch as she smooths the folds of curtain against the sill, as she tidies the cords behind the edges. She's wearing her smart herringbone suit, ready for work at the High School, where she is Librarian. My mother is in her coping mode, ever so gently but coping all the same. I know that she is trying to rescue me, but it doesn't feel like I am being rescued. She picks the clothes up again, goes to the door and turns back to look at me, as if waiting for me to say something, but there is a vacuum in the air, a challenge that she does not utter, and without it I cannot break through the inertia that has taken hold of me.

As my mother turns, I realize that she is wearing her new contact lenses, tiny hard glass saucers clinging to the surface of her eyes; the miracle that means she need no longer wear her thick black frames and pebble lenses in public, that no one at the High School need ever know about the ugly glasses she once wore. Without them her eyes emerge full-size, dark brown and beautiful, no longer quite Elvira's eyes but with the pupils smaller, less dilated, as if rationing the amount of light allowed in.

Mr Buchanan may have a job at the Central Library, she says as she goes down the stairs, if I ask him. Would you like me to ask him?

I pull the covers up around my shoulders.

Can you, I say.

In the drawer of my dressing table, in a smart pink ceramic case, is my own pair of contact lenses, each floating in its pool of sterilizing liquid. My mother bought my lenses at the same time as her own, although it is hard to see when mine will ever be worn. At the optician's I have failed to master the insertion process. Time after time I hover, bent over the hand-mirror laid flat on the table so I can see what I am doing, the lens perched on the index finger of my right hand and my left hand shaking with the effort of holding my lids apart; but every time I bring my finger close to my face my snapping eyelids flick the potential intruder away. Only after many failures, when the kindly optician has taken the lens from me and slipped it in the blind white of my eye while I stare off to one side, do I see myself unblurred in her mirror. My attempts to insert the lens are clear on my face, my swollen boxer's eyelids like a red shelf overhanging my eyes, my cheeks grooved from the pressure of my nails.

The optician says it is just a matter of practice, but, at that moment, I do not believe her. I don't believe that I will ever manage this thing, this forcing of a foreign object into my body, I will never manage to do what other people find so easy. Back home I push back the covers into a roll around my feet, but by the time I have got myself ready for the day, the front door has closed behind my mother, and I am alone.

I want to tell John that some part of my negative got trapped in the enlarger, didn't make it through the trays of chemical to the print. Something to do with the third dimension, but I'm not quite sure what.

Instead of university, I am to have a husband and a job; adult things that come upon me all in a rush, like the proposal of marriage my prospective husband makes after only six days' courtship. From the inception of our relationship, when I sit on his knee at a party in my mother's altered wedding dress, the best part of a half of Booth's inside me, and utter the immortal words, I fancy you, we are committed to one another. Our cultural lack of fit, which will eat away at our solidarity in the years to come, is in the early days mutually strange and exciting: for me exposure to the loud and uninhibited Ukrainian family from which Peter longs to escape; for him, my parents' dignity, the books, art, music that inhabit our lives. We become symbionts, each offering something that the other needs. Exchanging background for background, I start to get drunk often in the student room with its orange lampshade swinging gently a foot above the floor, feeling the alcohol loosening my voice until it hangs as slack as the voices of the other students, drinking myself free of restraint, of decorum, of the good manners I grew up with.

All this my mother watches at a distance, in some alarm. She likes Peter, whose middle-class aspirations and quietness reassure her, but she is dismayed by the speed of our engagement.

They're not our sort of people, she says when pressed, and the slight hauteur in her voice allows me to dismiss the concern.

One evening, in the dim light of the students' television room, I become weary of squinting at the screen, of following the programme through sound alone. I take my glasses from my handbag and put them on. They are no longer the black-rimmed sixties style but softer, gold-rimmed, lighter on the face.

Peter turns, smiles at me, and approves.

They make you look intelligent, he says, and I am not even offended. I feel as if I am going to be safe at last. Our courtship, and the word fits, is old-fashioned, even innocent. We discuss the things for which we are, as yet, unready, the idea of children being one of them. Not yet, I say, not until we're older. There is a tremor in my voice as I say this, but no anger, no reaction from my fiance. Just the quiet, measured acquiescence of someone who is calm, who has no hidden anger, who is oddly like my parents.

We marry, to my mother's relief, in Wilford Church, posing for our photographs outside the door where she stood with my father twenty-seven years earlier. Even the pose is virtually the same: the bride's right hand tucked into the crook of the bridegroom's left arm, his right hand reaching across his body to hold her emerging fingers. The bride smiling, all in white. But where my mother stood firm and upright I am tipped on my axis, leaning slightly against my husband; my head tilted to one side. I am twenty-one, and I have just left home.


In my new job I am surrounded by books, thousands of them, books that pass through my hands unread. I work with three other girls in a basement office of the city's Central Library, checking orders and unpacking boxes and processing new stock for the libraries. Our responsibility is solely to the outsides of the books: we attach white labels with ruled lines for the ladder of date-stamps they will accrue, we produce sets of catalogue cards on an unnerving machine where the cards must be slipped one by one onto a glass plate, before the metal head with its black inkpad punches down to print them. Throughout the miners' strike of 1973, in an office with no natural light, the book ordering clerks work by the hiss of gas-lamps, using the plating and printing machines as the power comes on by rota. When there is no power, we strip the dust-covers from novels and sheath them in plastic jackets, so that the books feel sealed and clean and glossy to the touch. I get used to the dry-leaf smell of paperbacks, to the dense, smoky weight and polished pages of illustrated hardbacks. The books are 'finished off', as the office phrase has it, wheeled from the book ordering department on a trolley to the library van, which waits to take them out to the branches; to the readers of the books, who are somewhere else.

For a long time I do not miss the words. Library work is genteel, an apprenticeship that my mother has served before me. And I continue to invent a life, invisible and silent for now, a life that is somewhere else, somewhere in the future. I tell myself and other people that my job is just rehearsal: I still intend to take my degree, probably by correspondence, as soon as I have time. But the truth is that the working world is consuming me. It is as nearly an all-female world as that of school, and with fewer consolations: no exams to pass, no best friend, no darkroom. In 1974, as local government is reorganized, the City and County Libraries merge, and there are two people for every position. The politics of the time preclude redundancies, but there is a scramble for positions of power, and the City staff, who are moving to strange premises at County Hall, come off worst.

County Hall means an end, for now, to the Toll Bridge crossing and the bus trip into town. Instead the walk to work becomes the old route to the dentist's, the elevated floodbank path above the Willowwoods, two rural miles along the curl of river to Trent Bridge and the great brick barracks with its turquoise copper roof. Our new light office block is an extension to the council building, hoisted up on concrete stilts above the car park, with a view of the grey smooth river unwinding from its Wilford loop fifty yards away.

A year passes. The golden summer of 1976 burns down out of an empty sky. Leaves crisp on the trees in August, the Willowwoods bleach into prairies of straw criss-crossed by brown crazed paths, standpipes march north across the country without ever quite reaching Wilford. Three miles away, at Clifton Hall, a plume of grey smoke rises into the haze. The Hall has closed as a school for ever, and a group of old girls are burning a paper phoenix on the seared grass of the top playing field, with an off-duty fireman in attendance to dowse the thin white flakes of ash. At County Hall, at a desk below a wall of windows, I sit and carry out my work. I have been inaugurated into the office regime of diets, and every lunchtime the girls and I take our one-cal Cokes and lie out at the sun's zenith on the grassy bank above the river, smearing our legs and shoulders with Bergasol, a new miracle suncream that accelerates tanning, forcing our skins through a roasting scarlet on their way to brown. The river stinks with a toxic algae that has bloomed in the heat; there is scum on the new low-water mark on the Victoria Embankment steps, and the fishermen are avoiding the place, as are mothers of small children.

Back home, in our new garden beside the churchyard in Wilford, the leaf-canopy is still dense and green. My husband and I do not quite live in God's house, but something close to it, the servants' wing of the Georgian Rectory, where our landlord is the minister who married us, a kind man with Roman nose and calm, long-sighted eyes. Our rooms are full of light from the great sash windows; we tiptoe into attics with dormers that look out over the loop of the Trent and the formless city-spread beyond, but leave undisturbed a secret room whose boarded door is halfway up the attic stairs, and whose round window peers one-eyed from the rear of the Rectory across the dense foliage of our back garden. The ancient cherry trees cling together to save moisture, while every evening my mother walks up from the avenue with a pail of vegetable water to pour around their roots. Looking up into the canopy I see that the cherries have fruited red, well out of reach, as if to mark Wilford's Flower Festival.

The thick grey line of heat rises up the thermometer. Blinds are clattered down first thing at work, curtains pulled across bedroom windows before the sun can focus on the lens of glass. On one of the hottest nights of the year, my mother is woken in the small hours by my father, moaning in agony at the pain in his stomach. The out-of-hours doctor is a stranger, and leaves it to my mother to decide if the symptoms warrant an ambulance. A day later my father has been operated on for perforated ulcers, ulcers that have probably lurked inside for years, gathering strength at each new instance of my father's gentle neuroses: his obsession with punctuality, with the military arrangement of his clothes, his precise calculations of the family's finances. My father recovers from his operation, but he has been frightened, and when we visit him he is already edging himself away from hospital, sitting forward on the chair beside his bed in his check dressing-gown, his shoulders hunched away from the high chairback as if to lean against it would be to invite relapse. His one desire, he tells my mother when he is finally back home, is to get back to his routine, to resume his life exactly as before.

But life is not as it was before. I no longer live at home, and my mother is reporting what my father has said over the phone.

And my heart sank, she says; and then she pauses, as is her habit.

And when he retires, she says, he's going to do nothing.

There is another pause, but this time I can hear the white words in the silence. My father's illness has drawn a blind back on the future, and my mother has seen her life down the years alone with him and his routine. Not leaving him, not raging, just enduring in a silence unmediated by my presence. I listen to my mother's words, but at some kind of a remove. I am thinking of the gently musty smell of silence in my parents' house, the cool quietness that hangs like lace inside it even in a summer like this. My parents' house; not mine, not any more. I twist the coiled cord around my hand, as if I could reel myself back in.

The sky begins to whiten as the summer exhausts itself. It's still hot, too hot for my favourite trouser suit, a rust-coloured three-piece with my silk striped going-away blouse. Today my hair is greasy so I've tied a crepe scarf round my head with the long ends trailing out behind me. I'm walking home, just after 4.30, the two miles back to Wilford along the river. At some point I should meet my mother, cycling along the floodbank to meet me. We have a loose agreement that she will come out to escort me home when I leave early, since Peter does not leave work until after five; although I know the nervousness about the river walk is mostly in my mind, as my mother has walked this path, accompanied and alone, a thousand times. From the County Hall end the path starts on the open riverbank and then disappears in a narrow stretch between a high wall on the left and the hedges of the riverside gardens on the right. It has the feeling of a railway cutting.

Just before the hedges start and cut off the view across the river, the right-hand boundary of the path is marked by a line of railings, yellow paint peeling from their rusty bars. As I approach, I see that there is a man leaning on the railings, looking at the river.

He does not look like anything much. Dark, sunglasses, droopy moustache, and a shopping bag over one arm. I am past the railings and onto the narrow stretch of path, with the high wall to my left and an uncut hedge on my right, when I hear him running. He jumps on me from behind and I scream. Then he has his left arm round my neck and he is saying, Shut up, shut up or I'll kill you. And with his right hand he grips my right hand and puts it down his trousers, telling me to get on with it. And That's right, he says, a few times. That's right.

My back is forced against the wall. I feel the grit of its rough concrete, the roughness through my clothes. I can't see anything in front of me except the long whip-stems of uncut privet with their scorched cornflake leaves. And the feeling of this greasy tube of flesh, like uncooked meat, dead in my hand. There is just that and the weight of his arm round my neck, and the not letting go.

And then I hear a voice. A female voice, speaking from somewhere above me.

131

Did you hear a scream? the voice says.

Behind the wall, built high above the riverbank, is a line of white-painted houses, Victorian mansions with turret rooms and balconies mostly used as offices. Some window-sashes are pulled right down to seal the rooms against the river-smell, but one or two are open for the heat. And somebody answers the first voice, somebody saying Yes, they heard something. Then the scrape of cords on timber as a window is pushed right up on the first floor of one of the turret buildings, and two women leaning out, their voices slicing through the haze.

Yes, down there, the first one says. Can you see?

And suddenly the arm lifts off my neck. He's let me go and he's running again, back the way I've come towards the Suspension Bridge.

I fall back against the floodwall. The concrete is broken up every so often with barred iron gates and steps, for access from the buildings to the path and river frontage. There is a clunk and jingle of unlocking as the two office workers who have heard me open up their gate to let me through, take me up to the office, give me a cup of tea, phone the police.

They say, Are you all right, and I know they mean, Did he rape you.

Yes, I say, I'm all right. And I drink my tea.

Then they lean out of the window again, shaking their heads and saying Broad daylight, but they cannot see where the man has gone. The police come in a Panda car and we drive round the Meadows trying to see if we can spot him, but the one who is not the driver pushes his cap back to air his head and says, He'll have gone to ground.

And then they drive me home. Not back to the flat, where there is no-one at home, but to Vernon Avenue, to my parents' house. They wait until my mother answers and then they drive away. My mother appears at the door, her outline scattered behind the stippled, leaded glass.

Oh, she says, as she opens the door, I thought you must have left early, I thought I must have missed you so I came home.

And then she looks at me. What's happened, she says.

I'm all right, I say. I say it again, when the words won't come. I'm all right as long as I don't tell, not the whole of it, not what I did because he made me do it, because I didn't want to die. The rest of it I tell the way I told it in my statement to the police. I tell her he exposed himself, he threatened to strangle me, and that was that. And my mother is silent. Silent with her head bowed, her hand cupped over her neuralgia ear, as if she can only bear to hear half of what I am telling her. I can hear my own voice thrown into the coolness of the room, and all the time I am wondering how far from me she was when it happened: if she was a hundred yards away, further back, up on the floodbank with the bike ticking under her, looking round for me; if she heard my voice faintly, in the distance, and thought it was the squeal of a child across the river who had hurt her knee. It is only when I am walking back to the Rectory that I hear the scream in my head as I made it: clear, rippling through the sodden air, the voice I used in the click of time before he got to me, before he silenced me. Scream in time and you'll be saved.

## *11*

### *Wisdom Teeth*

I am all right. I say it again at work, when the girls gather round asking questions. I say it in the hope that somebody will see that I am not all right, that they will contradict me. But the weeks pass, and the subject slips from conversation. The library packs its bags and moves again, from County Hall back to the city, and my journey to work reverts to the Toll Bridge crossing. There is no need to think about, yet alone tread, the riverside path any more. In the new library, I am supposed to be in charge of daily office routine. But half the time I am absent, approaching the office manager with yet another request for time off to visit the dentist, absences that run into hours. Although nobody ever says anything when I return, a space is opening up between me and my colleagues. A sense is growing in us all that there is something wrong with me, something unconnected with dentistry; an unvoiced suspicion that my appointments are code for something else.

If they are, even I do not see it yet.


I am back at the dentist's. Not the childhood surgery, where as a child I screamed and screamed with the pain of the drill. You mustn't do that, he would say, but I did, I knew even then with childlike instinct that I was under attack. But nobody screams at the dentist's in the 1970s, or not anyone that I can hear. The modern surgery is more silent than it's ever been. Unless the patient fears the needle, there are injections to numb the mouth and stop the sounds that once shuddered through the folds of my mother's headscarf as she sat on the hard chair at the back of the room. The needle is humane, but deceitful too: it steals your mouth while flesh and bone are cut away, while specks of darkened tooth spurt into the room in the water-jet of the new high-speed drill, while nuggets of lead-bright amalgam are pressed squeaking into hollowed molars. At home, slowly the mouth comes back to life. By then it's too late to scream.

In my early twenties, my mouth is dark with the legacy of my teenage illness, dark with fillings in the teeth I couldn't brush for weeks. But at the very back of my gum-ridge, just before it softens and sinks into my jaw, new teeth are pushing through my gums: clean teeth, fresh and unspoiled, showing like white bulbs beneath red translucent soil. I can see them in the mirror when I open truly wide. My wisdom teeth are coming late; but they are coming.

The dentist sits back and removes his mask. His breath sours out in a small invisible cloud.

We might have trouble with these wisdom teeth, he says. We'd better get you into hospital and have them out.

He removes his instruments, turns his back and starts to write on a form.

Are they impacted? I say.

He mutters something I can't quite hear.

136

I shut my mouth, fold my lips in until they're pinching one another, and shake my head. The scream is lost deep down now where I can't even feel the echoes. I can feel tears coming.

Well, he says, it's up to you. But the longer you leave it, the worse it will be.

I sit up and spit the pink mouthwash into the flushing bowl. The receptionist is waiting with the appointments book, but I make an excuse about work, pull apart the Velcro collar of the blue plastic bib and slide from the chair. By the following week I have an appointment with my mother's private dentist, for a second opinion.

It does not occur to me to stand my ground.

I am sitting in the waiting room, trying to read House and Garden. I have been here an hour, and may be another hour yet. The length of time the private dentist takes with his patients is a mark of his care, but already I have been away from work since ten o'clock.

I look at my watch. My arms are aching, and the temporary crown at the back of my mouth is working loose. The new dentist has spared my wisdom teeth, but set to work on the rest. When the receptionist finally summons me into the surgery, the dentist is holding up my x-ray to the window. He points to the inky patches shadowing the base of every molar, shadows leaking from beneath my fillings into the root below.

I'm afraid there's been some very poor work done here, he says, and I am not surprised. Although there must be further treatment, what is suggested is not more fillings. That is the NHS way, the way of lowest cost and quality. Crowns, the dentist says, revealing a battery of real teeth, are the only answer. There will be whiteness again, a smile worth having. And as he turns his back and charges the syringe with cocaine I comfort myself with the thought that my wisdom teeth are exempt from this. Perhaps it is the dentist's certainty that convinces me I must be in good hands. Or perhaps it's that I don't know how to question certainty, how to raise myself from the prone position it has placed me in.

The work progresses. It is curiously like the work of the NHS dentist, except that when the process is complete it is new whiteness that appears in the mirror, a smoothness that my own teeth never had. I am not invited to see the stump of my own tooth before it disappears for ever. Or not for ever, because occasionally a temporary crown will pop off and have to be re-glued. What is underneath looks like the burnt stump of a tree; black, forlorn. I put my finger in my mouth and touch it; there is feeling there, but I can't tell if it is in my finger or the tooth. Behind the stumps, my gums balloon with the continuing eruption of my wisdom teeth, but I will not mention the pain. I turn up at the surgery week after week, while the dentist carves away at enamel and replaces it with porcelain, porcelain that comes with a price worthy of the sheen. What is in my mouth is no longer mine but the work of someone else, awaiting payment, payment that I cannot afford. I show the bills to my mother, who pays them without a murmur. And when I finally get back to work, hours

138

later, I find I am too late for the visit to the new computer room. The new girl has been taken in my place.


For the fourth time this week I have a headache. Or not a headache precisely, more a tightness right around my head, a feeling of pressure across my temples as if the skin was shrinking back against my skull. Under my hair I can feel bumps and raised, pulsing veins on my temples. In the newsagents' where the girls buy chocolate and cigarettes the headlines all seem to be of tumours and thrombosis and sudden, always sudden death visited upon the young; headlines that work themselves into my brain, that seem, in some sense I cannot understand, to be about me. I go back and forwards to the doctor with my mother, always fearing the worst. X-rays are taken, my eyes tested, my head poked and prodded. More money – again, my mother's – is spent on a comprehensive BUPA medical. Nothing can be found.

But the all-clear never convinces me. Today, like other days, I have a racing heart, pins and needles in my arms and legs, pinheads of sweat breaking out on my palms. My dark wet handprints fog the book-jackets, handprints that fade slowly into smears, like photograms in reverse. I go repeatedly to the toilets and open the window, breathing hard. The gush of air slows my heart for a while, but the pins and needles have got into my ears. There is the sound of the sea in my head, growing louder. I know that only one thing will help me.

I have to get out.

The door at the far end of the office opens onto eight flights of concrete stairs that lead down the spine of the building to the basement stack, where the older, rarely borrowed books are kept. Library staff occasionally come down looking for a specific book, but mostly the shelves are undisturbed. As I go down, passing floors, descending into the foundation of the building, my panic slowly subsides. At the foot of the stairs I open the door into the stack and close it quietly behind me. The air smells of old newspapers and damp soil. The fine moss tracery of dry rot spreads across the wall beside the door, putting out its black and green tendrils into spots of peeling paint. I can feel the sediment of the library settling around me.

I have been here before. Many times, in the past few weeks, when the girls in the office are turning their backs, when the pins and needles have become too much to bear. This is where I have started to read again.

And I am reading history.


Medieval history, specifically Dewey shelfmark 942.033: the reign of King John, the most reviled of all monarchs, a king whose reputation needs rescuing. And I am going to be the one to rescue it.

My mother has a book whose title has always intrigued me. *The Daughter of Time*, written by Josephine Tey in the 1950s, is a novel which redeems Richard III, the pantomime villain king of Shakespeare. Tey's protagonist is a bedridden policeman who refuses to believe in the murder of the princes in the tower because Richard's portrait is not that of a murderer. I have not until now given much thought to medieval kings and their reputations, but that is about to change. By the 1970s Richard III has acquired not only champions, but a whole society of believers; bad King John, by contrast, who is also said to have disposed of his nephew, has none.

I first encounter John as a young prince in a Sunday TV series, *The Legend of Robin Hood*, aired on the BBC in the late 70s. Robin Hood, despite his Nottingham pedigree, is myth, and the kind of folk-myth that does not interest me; that the received wisdom of history might also be myth is an idea that is new to me. History is not really my subject - I have not studied it even to O level – but I know that the received wisdom concerning Richard the Lionheart and his brother John is of Richard as the glorious hero-knight, John the scheming faithless brother, one day to be so reviled that even his name will be expunged from the list of those suitable for future monarchs. But it is the Robin Hood story, a floating narrative disconnected from recorded history, free from any responsibility to the truth, that is most potent in the legend of the evil king.

In an early scene from *The Legend of Robin Hood* the good and bad brothers are wrangling over the succession. Richard, about to mortgage England and depart on the Third Crusade, is listing the many reasons why John may not stand Regent in his absence. The words are those of received wisdom, but the images on the screen slide between them, smudging their certainty.

The crusader king wears a cardboard crown pressed uncertainly down onto a bed of ginger curls; he has sharp features and an edgy, petulant voice. John, by contrast, has a face straight from fresco, with languorous blue eyes and the lucid, beardless skin of an Annunciation angel. While John drinks from a jewelled goblet and tries out the throne, his brother pursues the catalogue of his shortcomings. John is idle, he favours evil counsellors, above all he has no skill in warfare: witness his failure to subjugate the tribal Irish. The word *failure* occurs, and recurs, but John's smile remains steady. The waves of his brother's accusations break on the smooth surface of his skin; within, the air is dark and dense. The gold-painted coronet gilds his hair like a shattered halo.

Richard babbles on, but it is too late. The lion-heart is a man of straw. For a significant moment I become Tey's policeman: this is not the face of the mythic tyrant king who killed his nephew in a fit of drunken rage. But it is not merely a question of innocence. Innocence and guilt are two-dimensional concepts, opposing sides of the same flipped coin. This young man with his medieval face and fresco stillness is not portrait but sculpture; only the outside is worked into smoothness. And it is the inside that has caught my dormant imagination: complex, hidden, an interior darkness into which I can vanish. I try his words out as if they were my own. The echo is like the sound of two voices. The sensation is heady, like the lucid stage of drunkenness. As the phrases cluster into sentences in my head I feel a surge of joy.

In the library basement I prise the books from the stack, feeling the rip as the unused volumes, jackets glued together, peel from the shelves. On the cover of the first history I read there is a photograph of John's marble effigy in Worcester Cathedral, carved perhaps twenty years after his death. The tip of the straight nose is broken off, the junction of the lips crumbled. It is the young man's face: bearded, broadened, but the same. Inside the book the king's plain one-beat name drums across the pages, the print set in an old typeface where the loop of the J swoops below the line. The name is spoken, over and over again. I feel the strength of it.

The door into the basement creaks. Someone is coming into the stack. I shut the book and walk quietly to the end of the shelves, slipping into the stairwell before I am spotted. Then I begin the slow climb back to the top floor, Dr Warren's biography of John held underneath my cardigan. Today, when I leave work, I will go out through the loading bay, to avoid the issue desk and the new white gateway of security screens. Once at home, I rip the date-label from the book's endpaper, pasting over the torn list of dates a coloured bookplate with a dragon spitting fire. Beneath the dragon's feet I write my claim: *This book belongs to Roberta Dewa.*

The girls are in a good mood. They have discovered a new diet in Cosmo that promises a loss of four pounds a week on a strict regime of 1000 calories a day. As usual, the whole office is roped into the regime, and anyone spotted taking solid food before lunchtime is reprimanded. Through the morning we sustain ourselves on black coffee and Sweetex, but the caffeine makes me sick and dizzy, and in my desk drawer I keep a packet of Ryvita and a tub of cottage cheese for when the nausea breaks out on my palms. Invariably, someone will hear the crackle of the packet when I dip down to my drawer, and call a reprimand across the room.

The office manager looks up from her corner.

I've got some orders to send, she says. Who wants to deal with them?

I look down at my work. Sometimes I remember that I am supposed to be in charge, but my promotion feels long ago and far away, displaced by the library's move back into the city, by my long blank absences at the dentist. Less often, I recall that I am eight stone two, and do not need to lose four, or even two pounds a week. Today I am meeting my mother for lunch, so I close my drawer and get my coat on to go out.

I glance across the office, where the girls are calculating calories for the week. I'll be back about half past two, I say from force of habit, but there is no reply, and I have the sense that my words die out before they reach the other side of the office.

I look at my watch. It is five to one, October 18th, 1977.

I go out through the front entrance of the library and emerge onto Angel Row just as Little John is striking one. The traffic noise surges up to me as the automatic doors slide shut at my back. The sea is still shushing in my ears, but it is the drumbeat of my heart, sounding in the hollow of my throat, that I can't ignore. Five past, ten past come, and there is no sign of my mother. I see the glassy echo of myself pacing up and down the shop-breadth of the library windows. My heartbeat is still accelerating, and the noise in my ears has amplified to a sizzling static. There is a scream ballooning in my stomach, but the sound cannot get past the thumping in my throat.

I stumble back into the library. There are two girls I do not know at the enquiry desk, making out brown tickets for new borrowers. I go round the desk and squat down beside them, hunching against the desk for support.

Can you help me, I say.

One of them turns and looks at me.

Oh, she says, Do you feel faint?

I feel a chair brought up behind me, knocking hard against the flesh behind my knees.

Get her head down, someone says.

I have my head down but it does not help. Then I see my mother, head shawled in her Paisley scarf, leaning across the desktop at me, asking somebody to ring for a taxi. I try to get up but the static has got into my legs; they are tingling, wobbly like limbs gone to sleep. Somebody makes crutches of hands beneath my armpits and walks me into the public lift; and then we are rising, back up the building to my own floor, where the Evacuation Chair, subject of many office jokes, is kept folded against the wall. I am aware of the girls leaving their sandwiches and helping me onto the plastic seat, of someone either side carrying me, still on the chair, through the sliding doors into the service lift, clunking down to the loading bay, where a Streamline taxi with its flashers clicking is waiting in Bromley Place.

I'm dying, I say to my mother. I'm having a heart attack.

She is facing forward, giving the driver directions, and shakes her head. In Casualty they sit me down on another plastic chair inside a curtained cubicle and I wait for the doctor. The drumbeat in my chest has slowed to walking pace, but the static in my ears is whiting out all other sounds; each minute I expect the white to shade to blackness, to pitch forward into a blank of faint. Somebody pinches my wrist for a pulse, nods through my mother's account of my symptoms, but no white coat and stethoscope comes near me.

The nurse lets go of my wrist, produces a crumpled brown paper bag and gives it to me.

Breathe into that, she says. And keep it up across your face.

She's just hyperventilating, the nurse says to my mother. Too much oxygen in the bloodstream. She needs to rebreathe her own breaths, to get the carbon dioxide back into her system.

My mother asks a question.

Oh, she'll be all right. Take her to her own GP for a thorough checkup when she's had a good rest.

I do not notice it at the time, but the nurse never speaks to me, never asks me how I come to be in this state. As I inhale the brown must of my dampening paper bag, the static fading from my ears, I feel a

146

remoteness from the world that is only half to do with my symptoms. I am remembering, from a TV programme on deep-sea divers, the high cartoon voices of those who have inhaled too much oxygen. I am twenty-three, old enough to ask what is happening to me, but all I can think of is that only a child's voice would issue from my mouth.


Well, says the doctor, writing out a prescription for Diazepam, I think it's time for psychiatric help.

So it begins. Hours ticked away in waiting rooms that are not clean and smart like the dentist's, but are furnished with scoured carpets and chairs cast off from old people's homes; rooms filled with nervous, distressed patients, their fingers clenched round cigarettes that tremble showers of ash onto the floor. At St Ann's Hospital there is a woman with long purple nails and a face deep-cut with lines who has been in and out of psychiatric wards for twenty years; at Regent Street a young man with a hood of stringy hair who asks openly if anyone has any tranquillizers. Some are coughers, some pacers, some moaners. Some have pungent silences that pervade the room, leaking out of them like sweat. Nobody really talks to anyone else; it is all they can do to sit still and endure the wait. There is misery in all these rooms, misery that is half-contained and desperate and impotent. Forms arrive from the NHS requiring the patient to attend at Mapperley, at the City, at this or that doctor's clinic. Nerves and lives wear away in corridors where people wait to be assessed, to have their drug regimes scrutinized and revised; each time the regime changes the switchback of side-effects hurls them through another loop of nausea or dizziness or palpitations, each time they feel less and less participants in their own lives, increasingly invisible beneath the thickening shell of medication.

It has been established early on that I am not mentally ill, in that I am not schizophrenic, or bipolar, or psychotic, only nobody makes this clear to me. On the other side of the desk, the psychiatrist, with his shock-wave of white hair and Freudian fundamentalism, is clarity itself. *Over dependent on the mother*, he writes in my notes, and *suffering from psychosexual trauma*. He drags my husband into the clinic, and finds him *reticent and resistive* to discussion of our personal problems. As a couple we are referred on to another specialist; a new drug is suggested for my symptoms, one that comes with an impressive list of side-effects. The notes are summarized in a two-page letter to my GP, part of the medical file I will not see for thirty years.

But I do not take the drug, and I do not, quite, fall apart. Something protects me, holds me clear of the descent into psychic dismemberment I see in the waiting room. Though I do not see this clearly at the time, it is the sense that I can take refuge in a life that is not mine, played out in a time and place to which the doctors and their associates have no access. But just as nobody reassures me that I will not suffer the long fall into madness, no one explains the bodily symptoms my brain can not dismiss. I have never heard, nor will I hear for years, the phrase *panic attack*; and years more before I learn that other people suffer from the terrifying symptoms that seem the outliers of a rushing death.

Even if I knew, it would not help me at this moment. If fellow sufferers – those who know what a panic attack is like – are unfit for friendship, so too are my colleagues. I never go back to the office, and the girls, who I have worked with for three years, do not trouble to ask after me. Somebody organizes a get-well card, and there our contact ends. When I am gone the dust settles, in the office and the stack, and the girls return to their business with the books: ordering, stamping, labelling, packing for the vans that deliver boxes of glossy, tightly jacketed novels to the branches, words for someone else to read.

## *12*

## *The Daughter of Time*

The hypnotist is counting backwards. As he counts, I focus on the lava lamp that stands on the table between us. I watch the globes of orange jelly drifting up and down in the liquid, globes that do not stay spherical but stretch and elongate and reshape themselves into ellipses; mysterious as sea-cucumbers or jellyfish, creatures drifting passive on the current, whole and living in the water but flat and dead on the beach.

Close your eyes, says the hypnotist and, slowly, I let my lids shutter my eyes. For a minute the globes move on the dull red background like dark suns.

Now, he says, gently, Let's remember what we talked about last time. We talked about Granny Bailey and her Parkinson's, and how we were sad and lonely because she can't speak to us any more. We talked about your mother and father, who don't know how to help with panics. And we talked about the man on the riverbank, who has ruined married life for us. Can you remember all this?

I nod. Of course I can remember. I think of my grandmother sitting in her rigid chair by the living-room door in her bungalow, her arms placed dead-straight along the wooden splints of the chair-arms where they will not shake. I see her smile and raise one forearm with an effort to greet my husband, whose warmth comes over to her without words. I see myself, gritting my porcelain teeth on my embarrassment, holding the very ends of her fingers, dreading the moment when she will try to say something to me.

I think of my mother sitting halfway down the stairs of the Rectory Flat with her arms folded and her back to us, while my husband and I argue upstairs; my mother refusing to go home until the voices are lowered. And I think of her cycling along the riverbank path to meet me from work, the wheels of the old bike bumping on the crusty tarmac; I think of her looking ahead, around the indigo curl of the river, and not seeing me; standing for a minute while the pedals freewheel backwards, then turning the bike by its handlebars and cycling back to Wilford, while my one cry for help travels through the air and shivers into nothing before reaching her.

And you remember, says the voice beyond the lava lamp, how I explained that hypnosis is the only answer to all this.

I drop my chin. Through a slit of parted eyelids I can see the hypnotist sitting opposite me, his hands making an arch in front of his face with the fingertips touching; dapper in a velvet smoking jacket, yellow silk hanky hanging like a tongue from his pocket.

And what we need to do, he continues, is to go back to the place where things went wrong. Where we can relive what happened to us; and begin the work of repair.

I take in a breath and begin, yet again, my account of what happened the day of the attack.

The story will be truthful and convincing, so far as I can make it; complete with frowns and silences and real tears. But it is only counselling with closed eyes; not even that, because I am pretending, just acting another role. The truth is that nothing happens when the hypnotist counts backwards, a truth I have not yet found the courage to confess. Whatever he believes, I know that in the surgery the deeper levels of my mind remain untouched, the defences of my conscious mind unbreached by his techniques. My subconscious is off limits. It is busy somewhere else.

I have bought myself a notebook. In its pages I note down every scrap of evidence I can find in my history books for King John's defence. I learn about the loss of John's continental lands in 1204. I study maps of Normandy in the twelfth century, maps snaked over by arrow-headed lines tracking the king's campaigns to recover his losses; tracking his retreats to England, where he stands routed and defiant, fending off the forces of the French like the Union Jack in the titles of Dad's Army. I learn about scutage and baronial discontent and a suspicious king who, year by year, strikes off names on the list of those who can be trusted, who hires mercenaries with the coinage of ever-higher taxes until the baronage unites around the colourless standard of civil war. I see John's itinerant army lifting the siege of Lynn; I watch as the baggage train, unable to sustain the king's furious pace west, takes the shorter route across the Wellstream estuary. I see the gleam of a coronet as it slices into the tidal mud, a brown heave of the estuary as men and wagons and exchequer chests follow the treasure down, as silt and tide settle over the reign of a sick king who will fight his way to Newark Castle but no further. As dysentery takes hold and the body is voided of its fluids the once-lucid skin of the young prince is drying into grey pitted stone, hardening to effigy while the River Trent, a mockery of water running just below the castle wall and visible from the king's apartments, draws the grey last line of his life.

The door into the reeking chamber opens. It is the king's mistress Catherine, come to keep faith with him even unto death. She is there to bear witness, to proclaim John's innocence of the murder of his nephew. Unlike Tey's detective, she was present at the moment of Arthur's death. She was there, she says. She saw.

Here the narrative ends, but not the novel. To ensure that Catherine's truth is carried unmediated back into the present day, I have split her in two: one incarnation in John's time, one a self reincarnated in the present day, regressed into the thirteenth century to discover the truth, and transmit it to the present. Twentieth-century Catherine is a history student, ill at ease in the 1970s; her only inheritance from her former existence an unexplained but consuming obsession with King John, until she is regressed into his time. I put myself into the novel without any trace of awareness.

Following the king's death, thirteenth-century Catherine's work is done, her truth told. She gives up her body to the river, looking forward to an afterlife, in the sure and certain belief of a reunion with John after death.

Twentieth-century Catherine remains, marooned in the present, suddenly disposable. I do not know what to do with her. She visits the ruined gatehouse at Newark Castle, the scene of the king's death, but the ruins are barred by a paling fence that separates the visitor from unsafe masonry. Beyond the fence, high in the roofless structure, is the only place where she feels her life had meaning – the chamber above the gatehouse where, on a dark October night in 1216, she comforted the dying king.

I do not know what to do with her. So I leave her there, rattling the bones of the fence, facing down the centuries that separate her from the king.


Six months later, I receive a letter from publishers Robert Hale, to whom I have sent the manuscript of the novel. Their assessment is that the historical material is *powerful, passionate and very original*, but the present-day sections *somewhat disjointed*. As the story stands, a mixture of contemporary and historical events, it would be difficult to market, but if I am prepared to recast the novel as wholly historical, then they would be happy to see it again. I write back by return that I will do whatever they think best, and set to work immediately, tucking away my orange notebooks in a folder, and placing the typed manuscript for editing in the centre of my desk. I excise present-day Catherine from the narrative almost with relief.

In 2008 I return to Newark Castle for the first time in thirty years. The paling fence has gone, and what remains of the castle's interior has been restored and opened up to visitors. But in the twenty-first century, visitors are not allowed to wander unsupervised through dangerous places, subject only to the whims of imagination; rather access is strictly controlled, consisting of a fully guided tour of towers, undercroft and dungeons. The guide for the morning's dungeon tour is a wiry Ranger who steers our small party (myself, my husband, a mother and two children) along dusty corridors, through trap-doors and down steep oak ladders to the sealed barrel-vault and bottle dungeons. The Ranger chivvies us down the ladder into the blind circle of the bottle dungeon; he tells us how the barrel-vault is haunted by ghosts who, after rain, fling invisible coins and stones at visitors. He reminds us of the meaning of *oubliette*, inviting us to picture the strata of bodies within the dungeons, some pounded down to melted flesh and bone, some – his voice is flat, as with too many repetitions – still alive. The children screw their faces up and scream when the Ranger turns the light out, but I merely stand back and listen and let the flow of words slide past me. I tell myself that this is no longer my territory. I am merely visiting it, looking at the after-image of something that ended long ago.

But after lunch, the family has disappeared, and my husband and I discover that we are the only visitors booked for the second tour of castle towers and undercroft. I envisage a stilted, embarrassed trio, but as our guide locks and unlocks doors and we all trudge up spirals and disentangle the patchwork of architectural eras in the stonework, a slow peeling of awkwardness takes place. At the roofless top of the gatehouse spiral, where it's possible to look down on the shell of the room in which, we are agreed, King John died, I finally confess a particular interest in the king.

I'm not a historian, though, I make clear. Research, for a novel I wrote about King John some years ago.

The Ranger nods. Neither approval nor disdain.

But something will not let me leave it there. I realize I do not like the sound of *years ago*. I try again.

Actually, I say, I'm a bit of a partisan. I've always thought he's much maligned.

Another nod, this time accompanied by a glance.

Oh, I'd agree with that. In the literature nowadays it's pretty much accepted.

More keys, more doors and stairs. The Ranger and I exchange dates and abbreviated facts: 18<sup>th</sup> October, a surfeit of peaches and new cider; we dispose of the theory of the king's poisoning. Down this time into the cool marine damp of the undercroft, whose neat interlaced pattern of arches almost replicates the crypt at Worcester. The beach-damp sand floor of the undercroft and the tart green smell shows that we are at river level, close to the watergate where boats would have unloaded supplies for the castle. Here Catherine would have come after John's death, the sand like a border of ermine on the hem of her dress, through the low arch of the watergate down to the river. Laid out at our feet in the sand is another arch, its individual stones decorated with studs, chevrons, castellations and rosettes, the sundered fragments carefully numbered and arranged into concentric circles. The Ranger squats down to show us how he is re-assembling the arch, stone by excavated stone, a relic from the Norman castle which will be reconstructed in the Tourist Centre.

The arch is a thing of beauty, lying prone in the sand. I imagine it whole again, raised to the vertical in the Tourist Centre, incongruous against a plasterboard wall but safe from Newark's rougher element. Oh, yes, it'll have to be inside, the Ranger says wearily, and we nod.

On our way to the southwest tower where, we have agreed, King John did not die, the Ranger asks if I am aware of the recent theory that the king did not make it to Newark at all, but expired on the way at a village whose name escapes him.

157

No, I say. And suddenly I am in the king's death-chamber again, with Catherine in her sky-blue gown, barring the door against John's enemies. My neck and teeth set rigid.

I've got the correspondence in my office, says the Ranger, if you're interested.

The office is not like other offices. It is a chamber in the north-west tower of the castle, with a Tudor fireplace and medieval stonework in the walls and a resident ghost, captured by the CCTV as a soft white ellipse beside the desk, an image printed out and pinned to the noticeboard, alongside flyers for castle events investigating the paranormal. While the Ranger searches through his folders for the correspondence I read a couple of the flyers. There's some powerful activity here, he says without looking up.

The correspondence consists of a speculative history paper by a local historian, and a letter from the Ranger commenting on the theory. I skim-read the paper on John's death. Its account of the probable details of the king's illness is thorough, unpleasant and remorseless, suggesting that his dysentery was too advanced to have allowed him to reach Newark before he died. Then, more slowly, I take in the Ranger's reply, which dismisses the writer's argument on the grounds that, as the king's itinerary, and chronicled sources, make clear, the king died at Newark, in the room above the gatehouse, some time on the night of the 18th of October 1216. There is no need to read further. John did not die out on the highway, untended and unshriven, his body bleeding away onto the ground. As I close the folder, I nod and smile, biting my lip on the rush of gratitude that would embarrass us both. We go out into the daylight and the Ranger double-locks the door and the barred gate which protects it, before directing me to a couple of books on sale in the Tourist Centre. We shake hands and I thank him for his trouble.

No problem, he says. It's nice to get someone with a genuine interest.

I take home the books, one of them – called *Guardian of the Trent* – showing a photograph of the castle wall facing the river. I look at the window in the north-west tower and picture the Ranger tapping at the keyboard, writing tetchy letters to other historians and keeping a watchman's eye out for the rougher element. It didn't occur to me while we were inside, but I can see from the photograph of the exterior that directly underneath the office window in the tower is the slit opening and bulge of masonry of the bottle dungeon. The *Guardian of the Trent* says that the thickness of the upper floors of the towers would have blocked 'noise' from the prisons, but the Ranger's voice is still with me, and I imagine the wind howling as it did on that night in 1216, and the dungeon ghosts rising from their prison to glide like fingers of mist through the walls.

I unearth an album of my own, strictly external, photographs of the castle from that time and I notice how flimsy the paling fence really was, thin wooden stakes held together with twisted wire, not much of a defence against the rougher element of the 1970s. In the album there are photographs of the tomb at Worcester too, print after print of that small stone figure with the curled hair and beard and the almond eyes. And postcards of the crypt with its white painted pillars and red carpet, images too distant for the viewer to pick out the engravings in their glass cases.

I appear on just one of the photographs. I am standing posed outside the cathedral, against the Norman doorway that gives access to the transept, my pink handbag with its freight of orange notebooks held out before me. My head is tilted to one side, my mouth set as if someone has just challenged my right to be there. And yet there is a steadiness about me, the stillness of a woman finally claiming her territory. I am just outside the open door, but inside the dark archway a light is on – distant, a dim bulb shining somewhere in the cathedral. As I scan the photograph I feel as if I can see something in the arch of dark space, an after-image not of a figure but of lines of handwriting: the sloping, disjointed prose that created present-day Catherine, the words that never made it into print. They resolve and clarify until they become legible. But they are in negative, white words against the dark of the doorway, finally finding a page that will reveal them.


I close the album. I blink, as I did when directed to by the hypnotist. The globes stretch and sink in their sticky liquid, find circularity and lose it again. The numbers count their way up the centuries to the surface and I am back in the surgery, pale winter sun spotlighting into the room. How do you feel, says the hypnotist. And, Wonderful, I say, turning my back on him, gathering up my things to go. *Dulcissime,* only where love is will I open my mind.

## *13*

## *Queenie*

The division bell rings in a new decade. We have voted out the seventies and the three-day week, picket lines around braziers and angry placards and grim comb-over shop stewards. On the steps of Number 10 Margaret Thatcher quotes St Francis of Assisi: Where there is despair, let us bring hope; where there is darkness, light. We open the suddenly ubiquitous champagne and toast the new age. Snarling, spitting punks yield place to dandy highwaymen in white lace shirts and tasselled boots, while beneath the lace female shoulders broaden to mimic the male silhouette. Lady Diana Spencer smiles out from the TV in her Thatcher bright blue suit, engagement sapphire glinting for the photographers. As I am driven to and from Carlton in our new green Sunbeam there are songs on the radio again: Queen's *Play the Game*, Bryan Ferry's *Dance Away*, Abba – curiously resistant to the upbeat pull of the age – with the melancholy *Winner Takes it All*. Against this soundtrack Bjorn Borg, most gentlemanly of tennis players, hears his good-mannered murmurs drowned out by the screams and tantrums of John McEnroe. A letter appears in *The Listener*, complaining that St Francis' supposed words are not even medieval. Something distinctly secular is at work, transforming the world from the inside out.

Even at Wilford, where for years the river loop absorbed the forward movement of the world like a boom, waves are breaking on the isthmus. Our clerical landlord is gone, and the choir-stalls are empty of black-capped and gowned choristers, while the organist who sat behind them has retired to a more rural parish. A drum-kit gleams beside the church door, its cymbals oscillating slightly in the disturbed air. The old hymn numbers vanish from the wooden board, and in the responses words fall even from the Lord's prayer that we learned as children: *thy, thine, trespasses. Hallowed* endures, a stubborn stone that will not be dug out. My mother kneels in a side pew on a hassock whose cover she embroidered in blue and gold, whispering the Authorized version to herself, while a thin air whistles off-key in the organ pipes. The community whose leading light she has been for so long hushes back against the church door, aligning itself with the new order. A History Society is started in which she, archivist of the Flower Festival only four years previous, will play no part. My mother is moving out to the periphery, an unknown region for which she has no words, no understanding.

Only at her own mother's sickbed is she still at the centre of things.

Granny Bailey is not struggling to speak any more. She is lying on the frozen side of her body, her legs crooked beneath the quilt, just her face visible in the valley at the centre of her pillows. When I make a final visit on a sultry day in August, her eyes are closed, a small o of mouth just open and her cheeks flushed rosy;

163

but there is a glossy tautness to her skin that is not healthy, not even unhealthy, but passed beyond those things. Beside the bed my mother squats on the floor, drawing mounds of dirty sheeting into a basket, bundling the bedclothes slowly, as if the action represents the only rest she is likely to get until it is over. Rest from weeks and months of buses into town and out again, nursing and bed-changing and listening to the heavy panicked spin of the washing machine while my grandmother weeps quietly into the tissue laid against her face.

You can talk to her, says my mother. I think she can hear you.

I have not tried to talk to my grandmother for a long time. Now, when I am convinced she cannot hear me, it is easier: easier to hold the beak of her hand and thank her for her birthday present: an electric typewriter, a wonderful machine whose power makes the words fly from its light, responsive keys, that will write the next story I have planned. The old Petite that typed my first manuscript has gone to my mother, who has put aside her sewing and used it for letter after letter to the NHS, the Red Cross, the doctor, requesting help. When help does not come, she writes an article about the sub-life of the carer, perhaps the first she has ever written: an article that does not complain but offers practical advice, for daughters everywhere, on how to cope with ailing parents. After both the Daily Mail and Express have politely declined the piece the little typewriter is put away, the blue carbon of the article still curled around its carriage, and my mother resumes her silence and her sewing; falling back, as she has done so often, on the Drama Group, her own creation.

Like my grandmother, Noël Coward has not waited to witness the vulgarity of the new age, but the Wilford Players will mount one more of his plays, albeit in truncated fashion; and not for the village, which barely musters three rows of audience these days, but for a local drama festival.

Although my mother is producing, and I have a small role, we do not discuss the play. *This Happy Breed* is not a love story like *Brief Encounter* but the saga of an ordinary middle-class family in the years before the war. First produced in 1943, it is an overtly propagandist piece, whose characters still embody the virtues of decency and stoicism and knowing one's place, but now preach those virtues openly in a world besieged by new uncertainties. In this threatened world there is no Laura and Alec, dignified throughout their secret love affair, but the vulgar exploits of the family's youngest daughter Queenie, a girl who spurns her mother's existence of make do and mend for a life of colour and excitement. Queenie has none of Laura's reserve, no talent for concealment; her style is brash and open and above all indiscreet. If *This Happy Breed* had been penned in the fifties by a playwright other than Coward, she might have escaped. But written into a play book-ended by the two world wars, Queenie is trapped. She runs with her married man to France, but is abandoned and rescued by faithful Billy, who has always loved her; and who brings her back, humbled, to her parents' fireside to be forgiven.

There are few lines for me as Queenie, and even fewer demands on my newly fragile acting skills. Even so, it is the humility I cannot manage.

My mother has had rehearsals under way for some weeks, but a festival representative, a solid woman in tweeds with a shock of springy grey hair, has visited Wilford, and is not entirely satisfied with the production. One dark Thursday night she gets up from her seat at the back of the hall, walks past my mother and comes up to the stage. The spotlights blank her upturned face but cast a fan of long shadows at her back, spilling out into the hall.

You're all looking cramped and uncomfortable up there, she says. Why don't we try the scene down here on the floor, where there's more space.

There is a silence. Then a scraping as my mother pulls her chair away from the centre of the floor.

Yes, why don't we, she says.

I look at Eric, who is looking at Barbara. Slowly we jump down from the stage onto the dusty parquet, into the empty space where the audience should be, and begin the play again. But four feet down and the light has gone out of us. We take prompts we have never taken before, we stand on our new marks and mislay our exits. Our guest moves among us, shifting bodies and reciting lines as they should be played, while my mother stands, arms folded and silent, off to one side. I freeze in the pose I have been placed in, flicking the pages of my script back to Act II, where Queenie plans her escape, where she decides that she will be different from her parents. But Act III is where Coward closes the circle, when he reels her in.

Is Queenie ready? a voice says from the side of the hall.

I drop the play-script on the floor behind me and move forward. Ethel, my stage mother, has her back to me, folds of sewing mounded on her lap. Her right hand rises and falls as she tacks a seam, drawing the thin line of thread tight with each stitch. Her hair is curled and pinned around the smooth dome of her head in forties rolls. As I wait she becomes aware of me, her needle stutters at the top of a stitch and the thread goes slack. She grips the chair-arms and twists sideways until she is looking at me. Dark greasepaint lines bracket her lips and cup her eyes but they are still Laura's eyes, years after Alec's memory has shrunk back into a pinpoint pupil.

Hello, Mum, Queenie says.

Ethel rises slowly, one hand clutching the sewing to her skirt. As she starts to speak tears blur her voice.

Queenie crosses the stage to her mother and they embrace. But over Ethel's shoulder Queenie stares outward, into the audience and beyond them.

And, Curtain! the voice off says.

The players disperse for coffee. Our guest turns to me, the smile hardened on her face.

I think we still have too many scenes, she says. I'm sorry, but I'm afraid we'll have to cut this one. The play needs a lot of tightening up.

I take off Queenie's hat and shake out my hair.

Oh, that's fine, I say. I wasn't happy with it anyway.

As I walk past her, I notice her looking at the book I have left splayed open on the floor. She flicks a stare at me and I stare back. I have my own book now, I say, but not out loud, not with my mother present. I sit down and the book stays where it is.

I glance at my mother, but she's not looking at me. She is marking the suggested changes in pencil on her play-text. After the rehearsal, I hear her saying that she knows the production is not as good as it should be, but she is tired, after the months of caring for my grandmother and going out to work all week. Our guest quite understands, and - lowering her voice – so very sorry to hear the news.

At home, my mother says it again, *tired*, as if the one word is all I need in order to understand what has happened; to acknowledge that it is over, the Drama Group, the years of Coward and costumes and Elvira. But she speaks the word so quietly, that I never hear the weight of it.

In the tiny office at the High School we finish lunch in silence. My mother puts her flask away, looks at her watch and tucks the red notebook in her bag.

We'd better go, if we're to get there on time, she says.

At the hypnotist's, the waiting room is cold and damp and the receptionist puts on the gas fire for us. The blue flames lick up the lines of dust along the burners and the smell of burning leaks out into the air. After half an hour, I get up to go to the toilet. While I am washing my hands I hear the hypnotist emerge from the surgery, and go into the waiting room to talk to my mother. He is offering his condolences, with all the time in the world, for my grandmother's death. He is sorry, very sorry. But now my mother will be able to get some rest. Perhaps, she says.

I go out into the hall and the bathroom door swings shut behind me.

Ah, here she is, says the hypnotist, and starts to lead the way toward the surgery.

I stand still and he stops. He raises his eyebrows and gestures toward the door with a stiff arm.

I have to tell you something, I say.

They both wait and look at me. There is no enquiry.

I've been pretending to be hypnotized, I say. I've never been hypnotized. Not once.

The hypnotist laughs.

Oh, you have, he says. Believe me, I have enough experience to tell. Patients are often convinced they haven't been hypnotized. It's very common.

The air tightens. Before, the squeezing seemed to be in my chest; but now it's in the air between us.

I repeat my words. And then again.

The hypnotist has stopped looking at me. He is looking at my mother, who is standing in the doorway.

Don't you think you might be mistaken? she says gently.

I shake my head. I feel the fingers of tears on my cheeks.

I think perhaps we should discuss this another day, says the hypnotist. When you're feeling less tense. We'll talk about it on Wednesday.

On the bus I am shaking again, shaking like Granny all down my arms and legs. I weep and tell my mother, over and over, that I have not been hypnotized.

I know you think you haven't, she says.

*You don't believe me. You should believe me, not him.*

I can hear myself shouting. The people on the bus turn round and stare at me and turn back again. My mother flinches and whispers, For Goodness' sake, can't you say it quietly?

. No, I say. No, I can't.

We go home unreconciled.


When the contract for my novel arrives, I note that the publishers have an option on my next two novels. I have only a hazy notion of the first of these, but I know that it will be set in my holiday paradise of Snowdonia, in the days of Llywelyn the Great; and that the central romance will match red-haired beauty Angharad with Welsh freedom fighter Idwal, a character not very loosely based on snooker player Alex 'Hurricane' Higgins. Higgins, at the time head-butting tournament officials and ripping off regulation ties with gusto, is a ranting, raving McEnroe with more charisma, and, like Robin Hood's Prince John, more presentability, his bad-boy image intriguingly allied with a waif-like physical presence: an elfin figure with silky tresses and shadowed dark blue eyes – already so fully fleshed a character that I merely shift his Belfast origins to Gwynedd, and transplant him in the thirteenth century. But unlike King John, Idwal offers me no factual anchor to which I can tether my story. A figment only, he has no medieval tomb, no deathbed chamber, no chronicled life; only his twentieth century self is real. Inside the story, which is suddenly harder to write than I expected, he floats free, no responsibility to received wisdom or any other kind.

The story creeps. The historical research that fed *Lackland's Lady* here feels distant and irrelevant. The past is no longer the kernel, it is in the way of the present, and the present is suddenly where I want to be: with Alex in the high melodrama of the 1980 Crucible final, watching as in frame after frame he chances and misses, draws level with Thorburn and falls behind again. In the afternoons, when the stream of my writing narrows to a hopeless trickle, I run videos of snooker matches. Alex potting an impossible green, Alex drawing on the cloudy oxygen of a roll-up, Alex twitching through yet another row with the referee, Alex crouching over his matchstick cue, his pointed face uplit by the green light bounced back from the baize. And beyond the light, the audience, ranked rows of heads and shoulders sloping up into the dark. Sometimes the TV camera rakes the heads and among the tranced male faces there are a few female ones, mostly on the distaff side of a masculine escort. At the mid-session interval the audience unfreezes and flows out onto the gangway steps, programmes and pens at the ready, clustering round the Hurricane until only the crown of his navy Fedora is visible.

Alex is unfazed by this. The minders that will one day keep the fans at a respectful distance are years off, and even when the game has been purged of cigarettes and booze Higgins will resist, leaving finger of a smoke-trail in his wake as he hightails it back to the pubs where his career began. In 1980 I wind him back and forward on my TV screen, watching him emerging every now and then from the bear-hug of his devotees, running the tape again, rewinding the fans back up the steps, fast-forwarding them down again. Never once does he become lost, never once disappear out of sight. I am fascinated by his sense of self, the actions and idiosyncrasies that are spontaneous and unselfconscious: not roles, not diversions to conceal something else.

There is a girl in red on the edge of the scrum, not punching her way in for an autograph but waiting, strapped into silver heels to give her height. Awkward yet somehow imperious, like Queenie, looking for a gap that's the right shape for her, where she can force her way in. As the audience fades away she is spotlit suddenly with her glossy programme held out in one hand, a biro in the other, the pen she's held so long sweating dark blue ink into her palms.

If Queenie had made it through to the 1980s, she would whole-heartedly have dumped 1970s grey and brown for the red she loved as a child, when it was just bright and not evidence of dubious reputation. She would have loved the new bold triangle silhouette, buying the red seersucker dress in Miss Selfridge window with the pencil skirt and splits at the thighs and the flash of black lightning, silver-edged, across the bodice; picking up the silver theme with glitter in her hair, patting palmfuls of it up to her sticky hairsprayed curls, adding fingerpads of glitter to her cheekbones. She would have gone to the TBI on Sunday nights to play her five selections on the jukebox, cried when John Lennon was killed but in a theatrical way, as if it wasn't really happening, listening to *Starting Over* with one black Lycra-clad leg crossed over the other, turning her head for the glitter-flash; all the time keeping the red seersucker in plastic for the special occasion she knew was coming. And – having outlived the playwright who kept her fastened to the page - she would believe herself finally to be rootless, outside history and free.

My old schoolfriend's car streams into the sunset. Ahead, the pink clouds from the cooling towers at Ratcliffe-on-Soar Power Station rise vertical into a rusty sky. Stevie Winwood on the car stereo: *While you see a chance*. The motorway runs smooth and straight southward and then we turn right into the half-sun where the headlights pick out white direction fingers on blue exit signs: one, two, third left for Hinckley. The Leisure Centre also is rootless like all leisure centres, with an upstairs bar and a balcony where Pauline and I can drink gin and orange and gaze down into the green pool below. Tonight's exhibition match pits the Hurricane against old-stager 'the Count' Reardon with his black hair and widow's peak. Our seats are in the second row, catching the penumbra of the green light; only just below us Alex sits with his cue in the crook of his arm, seeming to offer a cigarette over his satin shoulder. He flicks a tower of ash into the sponsor's tray, drags and breathes the smoke upward into the air as if expelling a genie and the smoke flattens out into mist-layers hovering above the table. The reds are racked and re-racked and Alex twists and chalks and bends to scoop potted colours from the pockets before the referee can get to them. The white heel of my shoe taps on the treads of the steps as I wait for the mid-session interval. The referee calls four-all and Alex is away before the rest of us can move. The Count raises his eyebrows as my heels clack down the stairs and out onto the floor. At the far corner of the breeze-block hall, behind the stands, a red door swings shut.

I follow. *Bang.* I'm in what looks like a school gym changing-room with pegs and lockers and a long wooden bench around the walls. Another swing door at the far side, another changing-room beyond it. Nobody in the room but Alex, sitting on the bench and drawing on yet another cigarette.

I hold out the regulation item for him to sign. He looks at me and takes it from me. He's thinner in real life, his face hardly broad enough to hold his features. As he hands back the programme he looks at me again and I start to explain that I am writing a novel, that I want permission to dedicate it to him. The explanation takes a lot of words, more words than he wants to listen to.

174

Come to the pub, he says in his hoarse Belfast whisper.

He tucks the black cue-case marked *Fragile* under his arm and takes off through the doors again. Outside in the hall he spots Pauline, loaded up with coats and bags, and beckons to her.

We're all going to the pub, he says over his shoulder. Your friend is going to wash my hair.

A throaty barking starts up behind the closed door of the Star as Alex hammers on it and shouts Come on Ralph, open up, it's Alex; eventually the barking recedes into the distance and a bearded landlord unlocks the door to admit the Hurricane and the long line of hangers-on and groupies that trails back across the road. We go to the bar to buy some drinks and Alex heads for the phone in the corner. He's ringing his wife to let her know where he is, the landlord explains. We'll get his drink, I say, and Ralph pulls a half-pint and tells us to put it on the machine.

The machine is a table with a black glass top in a side bar. Alex is already astride the stool one side of the table, pushing buttons and jerking levers and squinting around the cloud of his own cigarette smoke. From one side of the table rows of tiny white crabs advance across the black glass waving their arms; on the other side a squared-off green apple pans side to side, shooting at them. Space Invaders is Alex's idea of relaxation between the sessions of a match; the apple is a laser cannon and the crabs are waves of aliens that must be destroyed. Beneath the table Alex works furiously at the game and the table emits a *Star Wars* beep each time a crab is vapourized. The faster the cannon fires, the faster the aliens come and Alex punches at the controls; the hangers-on close ranks around the machine, nudging me against its corner.

A luminous red score appears on the glass and Alex takes a slug of beer.

I can't let you do this book, he says. I've got my own coming out. My life story.

I try to explain that my book is a novel, not a biography, but I know he isn't listening. New waves of crabs begin to march across the glass and the cannon is firing again. As the second game ends I see Alex looking sideways at the seersucker dress and the black and silver flash rising slantwise across its bodice. He gets up, tucks his pack of Embassy into the pocket of his waistcoat, and takes me by the arm.

Where's this paper you want me to sign? he says.

I begin to say there is no paper, but I'm being manhandled through the bar, through a dining room at the back of the pub with a single table where crockery and cutlery are laid for two, up a flight of red-carpeted stairs to a landing at the top; a landing that on the right gives on to a series of brass-numbered bedroom doors, and, on the left, beyond a blue door that Alex barges open without enquiry, to a bathroom.

We are going to wash his hair.


So did he say yes this time? asks Pauline.

I take a sip of the drink she's kept for me. I can still feel the water flowing over the backs of my hands, my fingers registering its temperature as it slots between them. I see Alex's head down over the turquoise basin, the spray rebounding from a pink pool of scalp. I hear him complaining all the time that the water is too hot, that the soap is running frothy streams into his eyes, while in the background is the throat-clearing sound of the scum pouring down the pipe. I feel the hug of the towel round his head, the warm draught from the dryer blowing loose hairs into the air like strands of spun sugar, strands drifting back onto my face. And I feel the redness on my hands from the burn of the tongs, trying to hold the steel away from his pale skin, learning not to tug, not to talk through the task of combing out, smoothing a curve round the nape of his neck.

I put my glass down. The orange has settled to the bottom of the glass and the first mouthful is all gin and tingles round my teeth.

Not yet, I say.

Pauline stubs her cigarette.

I think this is the last time I'm going to do this, she says. I don't really see why you can't just write the book without his say-so.

I have another numbing shot of gin. The Star Wars beep pings from the machine across the room. I look over and try to catch Alex's eye but his head is down, his face lost beneath the velvet brim of his hat. A blonde perches on the stool opposite his, one suede-booted foot aimed outwards, towards our table. The words *last time* freeze in my mind.

We'll stop him on his way back to the hall, I say.

Don't be stupid, Pauline says. For God's sake don't be so stupid.

I push the drink away. There's only orange left in the glass anyway.

We take up a position in the vestibule of the Leisure Centre, where Alex will have to pass through on his way back to the main hall. There is a sprinkling of fans just arrived for the evening session, and a few looks cast in my direction that burn my skin. It's not long before Alex appears, cue-case slung across his shoulder, blue Fedora pulled down almost to his eyes. He clocks us and weaves neatly through the surge but the door into the main hall opens towards him and in the moment he's brought up short I've made the few yards to his side, put a hand on his wrist. There's a reflex jerk as I touch his skin. I feel the volts running up my arm as he pulls away.

Can I just have a minute, I say.

He shakes me off and turns on Pauline.

*I've had just about enough of you and your neurotic friend.*

Come on, Alex, I say.

*No!*

Later, years later, I will realize how typical the over-reaction is of him, how many others have felt the edge of a fury they can't have done anything to deserve. But not now, with the audience cupped round us, somebody asking what's going on, the spotlight bearing down on my head like a peroxide burn. Alex says his piece again, but he can't say it quietly. He's screaming at me, the brim of the fedora six inches from my face. The

178

shiny hair I combed and tonged for him into the bob of a medieval pageboy curls round his chin; but the face is here and now, a face screwed and pinched and wary as a newsreel of the Troubles, the surface of his skin like orange-peel. He's close, too close, the grace and soft light of romance gone out of him.

Bang. The doors slam closed and he's gone.


I tell my mother all about it. All, all about it, weeping and sitting on my father's bed while she sits on hers, not looking at me but head down, hands tracing the swirls of stitching on her brocade bedspread. Just once she looks up and takes in the red dress and bleached froth of hair and the glitter on my cheeks and the thin plucked line of the eyebrows that were once thick and ragged like hers, like the eyebrows of all the Baileys.

It is not a look that disowns me, but one that tells me that what she sees in my belated attempt to be grown up is not what she once hoped for. *Not our kind of people*, as she said of my husband's family. I have grown out of the character she made for me, become a teenage rebel a decade too late, a young woman disastrously reversing the natural order of adolescence and marriage. And – just this once – she decides to pass judgment on me. It's hard to know if what she sees is Queenie, ever wanting more than she should need and breaking life apart in the attempt to get at it. Perhaps it's an attempt to shock me from fantasy into consciousness, to speak to the decent daughter who still must be beneath. But what I hear is Ethel, still contained in Coward's world, his words.

*Do you know how near you are to the gutter*, she says.

It's not like that, I say.

That night I put my face up close against my own mirror, close enough for my features finally to come into focus. All I can see clearly, before the edges of the picture fog out into a blur, is where the tears have dried into a ragged tideline of black mascara drawn across the slick of gold highlighter on my cheeks. Tears I seem to have been saving up for this day, flushing any words I might have written from the page. Only by the autumn of that year do the words touch paper again, and even then there is no novel there, just terse stuttered lines of writing on loose sheets of paper, writing I barely recognize as poetry; poems that start anywhere and end with trails of dots and dashes; but each poem dated, some weeks apart, some days. These are not mourning poems for Queenie's too-short life of colour and excitement, for Catherine, or the Angharad of the Welsh romance; they are poems written in the first person, scenes from my own life, the fragments of a story it is unsafe to tell.

As 1980 folds into 81, and the tears dry up at last, my hair goes back to its natural brown, my eyebrows grow again. Eventually, a new novel begins to form in my cloudy consciousness; still history, still medieval. Only this time, there will be no romance. No women.

## *14*

## *The Sound of Falling Chimneys*

The car dives into the dark. My back is turned on the steam-clouds rising from the cooling towers at Ratcliffe, a rose-pink forest tinted by the sun. On our left, above the high grey verge of the Bee Bank, Wilford's own, now obsolete power station looms pale on the dark sky like a negative, its two chimneys still needling the sky, twinkling like failing lightbulbs at passing planes. At the boarded village shop we turn right into the avenue. As the car swings right I try to think of the new novel I am writing, a novel whose story seems all at once cut out of cardboard like King Richard's crown. Only the poems feel real, the dated scraps of paper beneath the notebooks in my desk drawer. Raw and risky as diary entries, evocations of the green heat of the snooker halls, the seedy rooms and bars of the Star, the life I have tucked behind me with the fading steam-clouds. The car stops beside our house, the engine stutters, headlights flick off. The worlds I created in my head go out like stars.

And in the real world, the old Wilford landmarks too begin to fall, one by one, like a house of sepia postcards. Their obsolescence is trailed in the local paper: not only the power station, but the Toll Bridge too is scheduled for demolition, its wrought iron spans weakened into iron flakes so friable we could crumble them in our hands. The tone of the newspaper report is upbeat and businesslike: there will be a new bridge, in a year, a thin steel walkway slung between the old redbrick towers; until then the disused railway bridge a hundred yards downstream must suffice Wilford pedestrians for their river crossing. My father too is upbeat, pointing out that the closure will be in May, just right for his retirement; and he smiles the relieved smile that shows when he feels safe, that has been more tremulous since the days of his operation. We smile too, and make a joke about his letters to the council, and only later, in bed, do I think of the bridge that has carried my family across the indigo band of water all our lives, its lattice arms held straight out at our sides to guard us from the water, letting us down gently onto the cobbles on the north bank of the river. As I drift into sleep the grainy dark is like iron-red snow on the inside of my eyelids. Under the arch of the quilt I chalk the formula on the darkness with my finger.

In May my father slips quietly away from work, having saved up enough leave to retire two months before his $60^{th}$ birthday and avoid a retirement party. As the fields whiten with hogweed, contractors' vehicles rumble past the Ferry Inn and set up camp on the Toll Bridge approach. And on the north bank of the river a crane appears, fishing the iron piers of the old bridge into the air and landing them on the embankment, trailing them behind its chain like rusted ingots in the grass. Welders' torches spark late into the night, slicing them into scrap.

Three of us never witness the loss of the bridge. My husband and I drive in and out of Wilford via the crossroads, coming and going from the village without having to set eyes on the process of dismemberment; my father sits the days out in his armchair with a view of the concrete-framed back garden; doing nothing in his retirement, as he always promised. Only my mother, holding her job to her against a fall into the blank place at his side, must make the daily trip to town across the railway bridge, a sideways, thoughtful glance for the stranded brick abutments of the Toll Bridge upstream, red abrupt cliffs facing one another across open water.

In spring the new Toll Bridge is opened to walkers and cyclists, a mean span of steel barely half the width of the old bridge, too narrow even to meet the old abutments. The redbrick towers on the banks now fall into nothing, while a handrail funnels pedestrians to the walkway in the centre. A graceless bridge, a hybrid of old and new, jointed together imperfectly. Twin steel trestles straddle their new concrete piles in the river, their elbows poking awkwardly from either side of the walkway. And on the old brick towers, bright with the paint of restoration, the Clifton crest of an exotic bird – peacock or phoenix, I was never sure – still rises with ironic wings of resurrection from the baronial coronet. The Cliftons are long gone, the only phoenix I have ever seen the paper one we burned on the playing fields at the closure of our school. The painted bird's neck – now, for the first time, so clearly a peacock - arches with characteristic pride, a foolish bird as overdressed as Queenie.

## The Memory of Bridges

Just once that summer, out of curiosity to be where I have never been before, and before it too is gone for ever, I make the crossing of the railway bridge with my mother. Together we climb the temporary steps to the embankment, the scaffolding handrail cold on our palms. The gravel of the empty trackbed crunches underneath our feet. I know that far beneath the gravel, out of sight, is the bluebrick viaduct of the dramp, its cathedral vaulting mirrored in the pools scooped in the shaded earth; its arches still singing with streams of water. But up on the bridge, crossing the three spans above the river, a hard light presses down on us. On our right, the pendant tongue of a dropped white signal; in front, white daubs of gang graffiti on the central piers. Over our heads an open ribcage of steel hoops segments the sky.

I am light-headed, strange in this most familiar of places, hoisted up high where the trains once ran, where the good child I used to be must never go. A reflex crouches in me from those years, the whistle-sound of *trespass* that the church has tried to do away but I still hear, close and distant as the whine of wax-locked ears. I look back down the line to its vanishing point, then forward across the bridge, to the raw red walls of the rebuilt Meadows rising up on the north side of the river. No trains, no peak-capped God, no words between my mother and myself except for careful smalltalk. No roles to learn. No heroines.

# The Memory of Bridges

I try to keep on with my novel, but the heart has gone out of it. The women I have excluded from my writing seem to have escaped into the world, to be everywhere I go. Barmaids, shop assistants, my husband's work colleagues. I imagine that they threaten my marriage, that they are phoning to make secret assignations. They are bending across us, collecting glasses, they are chance-met in the street, smiling without cause. No longer characters, they are aliens, with glassy eyes and strange shut faces that I cannot read; but punching their way into my world, where in some fashion my husband must explain what they are doing there. Our arguments leak out of our house into the avenue, lucid in the night sky, while the chimneys loom grey in the darkness at our bedroom window, tense and condemned, waiting for the siren and the roll of dynamite. I wait too; stalled, my words trapped in a destructive loop of fear and suspicion, out of ideas.

On the other side of the avenue my mother is making plans for her life beyond the Wilford Players, beyond my father's retirement. Small plans, composite and compromise as the badly jointed bridge, but plans nonetheless, designed in the tradition of make do and mend to retrieve from her existence what is retrievable, and in the process to cause no harm. As she crosses the new steel bridge her bag is no longer crammed with Coward plays but novels: murder mysteries for her lunch-break, stories of crimes solved and the nap of the world smoothed back to softness by the skill of Lord Peter Wimsey. When she comes home there are small purchases in brown bags: tiny teasets in wood and earthenware, arranged on her bedside cabinet with miniature vases and glass bottles. And, more alarming to the rest of us, there are escapes, trips planned and carried out alone, without the family. A holiday, albeit in the company of the WI Choir, to Cornwall; as far west and south from Wilford as she can go and still remain in the island country she has never left. One Sunday, having excused herself from the family trip to the cricket, she takes the bus alone to an Air Show where Douglas Bader is appearing. When she returns her eyes are still following the curls and spins of the Spitfire. The nosedives, the flattening out before the ground. All night while it grows dark, while we watch the television, I glance from time to time across at her. Her eyes moving rapidly as they do beneath the eyelids in sleep, but wakeful, the whites flashing. She is flying, following the smoke-trails out across the river, heading south again for the distant sea-blue line.

And then, one evening in September, a late item on the news. Douglas Bader, the legendary flying ace of World War II, has collapsed and died after speaking at an evening party. Tributes follow, and a clip from *Reach for the Sky*; but no tribute from Kenneth More, the actor who fought for the part he said that only he could play. More's death has preceded Bader's by a month or two, but in any case he would have been past eulogic speeches; shaken into silence by Parkinson's like my grandmother. Some freight in the air keeps us quiet as we watch the clip: not Bader's plane crashing in the flames that cost him his legs, but his Spitfire soaring into the light.

I look sideways and think I catch a glimpse of Laura in my mother's eyes. A fixed look, not following the plane on the television but staring at a point between the base of the screen and the sewing-box below it. I have a brief image of her standing, in some unspecified time that predates my existence, held at the sea's edge; not the crumbled Cornwall coastline but the clean white-cliff stretch of Dorset. The pilot's scarf from the sewing-box is tied around her neck, the silk map of the countries she will never see a blur-line across the Channel.

The TV goes off. It's late, my mother says.

We say goodnight and wander home across the road.

One flat October day my father phones to ask if we can give him and my mother a lift to the City Hospital for an outpatient appointment. When we return to take them home, my mother tells us that she has to have an operation.

I am taken aback. Beyond the routine of my mother's neuralgia, I have no memory of her ever being in hospital, never even being ill herself; only of her attendance on others. I ask what is wrong.

Well, she says, it's a kind of blockage, in the intestine.

I frown, not understanding. Something in the word *blockage* that will not translate, that rebounds from my brain like Latin. In the car mirror my mother's hand is shelved across her eyes as the low sun flashes through the window.

Like food, you mean, I say.

Something like that, she says.

188

The car leans around the curve of kamikaze roundabout.

But you'll be out for Christmas, I say, for the holiday.

Yes, she says, I'll be out for Christmas.

I nod. I am thinking of the summer just ended, when my husband and I rented a cottage in the Lakes, our first holiday away from the timetable and forced company of boarding houses. The summer cottage is an island in a peaceful, somehow empty county that knows nothing of our troubles, our surroundings only cool grey lakes and head-in-clouds summits where my own brain cools and its arguments vanish into layers of soft hill-fog. Then and there we book Christmas in another cottage named for its blaze of azaleas; and as we drive my parents home across the twin concrete bridges of Clifton Bridge I face forward and hold the Christmas holiday in my head, the holiday that will calm and cure.

And my mother is behind me again, good as her word, as our green Sunbeam labours up the M6 in the weak light of the winter solstice, packed too tight with coats and boxes of medication and the great stone of a frozen turkey rolling at my feet. Azalea Cottage in December has no azaleas but a treacherous north-facing hill lane high-polished with a fortnight's ice. In the evenings, the three of us who need a drink help my mother down the dark lane to the only pub, where the barmaid looks over too often at our table, and the ghost of an argument ensues; in the daytime we muffle our throats and take short walks around the dark grey tarn above the house under a slate sky. On Christmas Day my mother rises early, cooks the turkey and rests on the sofa in the afternoon. There is no tree, no snow, no children or aunts or grandparents, nobody but ourselves, rendered down into the core of family we have become. My husband takes just one photograph of us as a family standing in front of the cottage, on the day of our arrival. My father and I stand outside on the patio, one either side of the half-open patio doors. My father is smiling, arms behind him, leaning against the door-frame; but my face is solemn, arms folded in front of me, my head tilted away as from something I don't want to hear. Between us, standing just inside the open door, so that she looks half-in, half-out of the cottage, is my mother. She too is smiling, her hands in the pockets of her cardigan, peering out from the darkness of the bungalow, her left side clearly in focus, her right arm visible behind the window but blurred from the Scotch mist peppering the glass. Slowly, imperceptibly, slipping out of the photograph into the dark interior of the cottage at her back.

On our last full day the weather relents. While my father sits in the car the rest of us attempt the first part of a mountain walk in the Langdales, with the winter spate of Stickle Ghyll roaring beside us. Not far up the valley my mother stops and leans upon her walking-stick and smiles into the ellipse of mist rising from the waterfalls. I turn and stop and smile too and ask her if she minds if my husband and I go a little higher. No, she says, you go on, and the smile is a real smile, she is not unhappy, we are not unhappy together. As we take to the path again I imagine that she is watching us, but when I look back she is standing just as we have left her, smiling and letting the stream-shower drift up onto her face.

We run south back down the motorway into the New Year and onto the new Clifton Bridge, the 1960s structure that has twinned itself without fuss or awkwardness to accommodate 1980s traffic. As we bear down on the city the familiar horizon is intact, the power station chimneys still standing. At home my mother talks of going back to work, she plans the layout of her new library in the evenings. I resume my place at my desk and try to work. One day I see her pass the house, going for a walk. She doesn't walk with trepidation but slowly, leaning on Grandpa Bailey's walking-stick. Her goal is the Bee Bank, a view of the chimneys before they are gone for ever, but when she gets there the slope is too much. Deliberately she turns, and begins the slow walk back. When she gets home my father has not shifted position, still sitting in his armchair.

No longer is there talk of my mother going back to work, nor even of extended convalescence. She must return to hospital for a second operation, as my father did seven years earlier. My husband and I are at home, getting ready for a Sunday afternoon visit, when my father calls an hour early. He comes into our living room. He doesn't smile. His head hangs stiff, still as a heron's.

Sit down, he says.

I stutter on my feet. What's happening, I say.

Sit down, he says again.

My father sits in our new Art Deco suite with the high curved arms. He does not lean back and rest his arms along the sides of the chair Sunday-fashion but sits forward in a crouch and closes his hands around his knees. He tells us that my mother has telephoned from the hospital that morning. Phoned to warn us, before we visit, that the doctor has told her she has cancer.

But, I say.

My father's head seems to get lower, his neck straining to hold it to his shoulders. Wait for the doctor, he says. Wait for the doctor.

The doctor's office is bright and white and full of papers. He is young and brisk with a cold disc of stethoscope bright against his coat as he perches on the desk-edge.

Oh yes, he says, Mrs Plumb's family.

We introduce ourselves and he nods.

I'm afraid there's not really anything more we can do, he says.

My father's head goes down and down, his chin sunk deep against his chest. He is crouching again, but this time his hands have slid between his knees, pressed tight together. He asks if my mother knows.

Oh yes, the doctor says. I've explained everything to her. She's an intelligent woman. I wouldn't have done otherwise.

There is a blank moment with nothing in it. The doctor shuffles off the desk-edge, as if he hears a call requiring him somewhere else.

I should tell you, he says, It will probably be weeks, rather than months.

I get up. Something is happening to me, something I recognize. My palms like hot springs, *ssshhh* in my ears, my heartbeat pumping in my throat. My legs buckle and my knees work as if I am treading water. Thick, opaque water; not shallow pale blue sea with sharp sand between my toes but indigo, bottomless river, water deep enough to suck my shoes from my feet. I stumble out of the office and punch my way through the swing doors at the end of the ward into the stairwell and pull myself, hand over hand, along the banister, my feet trailing after me, down the stairs. At the bottom of the stairs the long corridor that is the chief conduit of the hospital runs left and right. A wooden park bench, its dark toffee wood incongruous in the overlit rooms of the hospital, in front of me.

I sit down and slowly the sea subsides. The sound of the people passing along the corridor has the echo of a railway station where I've never been. I look left and the corridor diminishes into the distance, its strip of polished floor running straight as a die into infinity. Right, a mirror-view.

I am still there when my father and husband come to pick me up. My husband has explained what has happened to my mother.

I tried to warn you, she says.

At home I cry dry coughing tears and there is no story to make me stop. I cry at my desk in the smallest bedroom of our new house, elbows on the table, dry face propped on the crutches of my hands. At the hospital, when I visit my mother, I do not cry. I smile and tell lies that I do not recognize as lies. When she comes out we

193

will all go to the new Concert Hall together, we will get tickets for the Ice Rink to see the reformed Nottingham Panthers she loved when she was a girl. My voice is stiff and brittle and I struggle for something kinder, that will not bring the tears that have started to sound like retching to her bedside. And I resort to childish things, that I have never really put away. I buy a soft toy, a red squirrel, to give to her. The squirrel has soft red fur and tiny felt feet and hands and a label round its neck that says *With Love*. Inside the label I write in the character of the squirrel that I have come from the Arboretum near the High School especially to look after her. I write *My name is Fluffy. Please look after me*. My childhood self, strong at that moment, doesn't notice the contradiction. It doesn't see that I am split in two like the railway bridge, with dark water between my selves.

One day my mother is sitting up in bed, Fluffy at her side, her hands clasped round her knees. She says, I've had such a nice visitor.

The visitor is a new doctor, not the young man of the steel stethoscope but an older man, kinder and less precise, who has studied the young doctor's prognosis with a gentle shake of the head and, briefly touching my mother's shoulder, said We'll see what we can do.

As my mother tells us this I look at her, to see if this story is, like so many stories in our lives, told to us for my comfort. But in that moment it seems to me it is told for hers.

## The Memory of Bridges

We take her home. Wheeling her down the endless corridor that has an end at last in a gust of cool March air. We tug her gently from the wheelchair like legless Bader from his plane, and she tumbles, arms outstretched, into the front seat of the car. How helpless her own legs are we don't realize until we stand on the doorstep at Number 26, holding her upright by her hands, and she cannot raise her foot to mount the step. I cup a hand beneath the brown tweed muffling her elbow, a coat she bought for warmth the previous winter, a coat I disliked because it was devoid of her trademark elegance. Across the road the nets twitch as the three old spinsters who will outlive her by a quarter century watch as, somehow, we get her up the step and on to the sofa in the living room.

That night there is a documentary about Noël Coward on the television. My mother lies on the sofa as she did at Azalea Cottage and we watch the programme together until the whine of closedown and my husband and I say goodnight. Half an hour later my father rings. My mother cannot get up the stairs to bed, so can my husband come over and help. When he returns he says that they have carried her, one either side of a dining chair, and got her into bed.

Once in her own bed she does not leave it. On Monday the Marie Curie nurse comes and does what is necessary. My husband and I drive back and forth, fetching tablets and softer pillows and equipment. My mother lies back against the pillows in her blue bedjacket, draped over curves of bed and covers as if the very bones have left her. I sit on the end of my father's

195

bed and talk about the trips we will have and the arrangements I have made for hiring wheelchairs and she listens, mostly with her eyes closed, sometimes saying That sounds nice. She does not ask for anything, she does not cry or complain or call out. On Wednesday, my 29th birthday, she says

     I'm sorry about your birthday.

     And I say it doesn't matter.

     On Thursday morning my father rings to say that the tablets have made my mother sick, and the doctor has issued a prescription for liquid medicine; can we get it as soon as possible. Also a meal from Marks and Spencer, because she cannot eat what he cooks for her, and when he has asked her what she would like she says, Just some plaice, perhaps. We rush round but the Easter queues are long and by the time we get home it is past four. We're here, I say, as we come into the room, but though my mother's eyes are wide open there is a blind look to them. My father and my husband get either side of her to help her to sit up to take the medicine and nothing changes, there is no sound, no movement and then my father is saying Come on, Sheila, fight, and he is holding the mirror from her handbag to her mouth. And I am leaning against the windowsill and turning my head away, looking out of the window to the back garden and the railway embankment stretching out into the south. And gently, gently, they let her lie back with her eyes closed and her hands stretched out on the eiderdown and we are downstairs with my father on the phone to the doctor; and my father is saying We think, but we don't know, and can you come, please, straight away; and then the doctor is there, humming tunelessly as he makes out the death certificate and handing it over and looking at me as he says You did know, didn't you.

And I say, Yes.

When he is gone the Co-Op man is asking, very gently, if we would like to go up and pay our respects.

I go back up the stairs alone. She is sleeping peacefully, just as we left her, her eyes closed, her hands stretched out along the eiderdown. I stroke her hand and kiss her forehead and find the words that have gone missing so many years I can't even remember.

Downstairs, a letter my mother left for me. A letter she wrote before her first stay in hospital, in her strong graceful writing without a waver. She tells me not to panic. Not to grieve. She says she loves me. That she is proud of me.

We sit on into the evening while the garden outside the French windows turns indigo and finally my father leans forward in his chair and says

I can't go to the Ferry tonight.

And we look at one another and creep out to the car in the dark of the last week of winter time, drive out of the village to a hotel on the outskirts of town where nobody knows us; where until closing time we sit nursing our drinks, numbing our voices; whispering goodnights as we cross the road to go home.

In the morning, a blank at our bedroom window. The power station chimneys are down, felled just before my mother's death, a week apart; just the hollow finger of a stubborn stump left at the base of the older, smaller brick one; not even that, of the concrete chimney that

197

kept the black snow from the church and threw it high into the sky. In the paper, accounts of a low rumbling and a shiver in the ground as the chimney broke its back, powdering into a pillar of white smoke as it fell. Before each detonation, a wartime siren wailing through the air. Silence among the onlookers, the black crosses of remembered planes, the all-clear. White smoke dispersing on the wind.

Don't grieve, my mother said, and for a while I try, drunk as a prizefighter every day until and including the funeral. My mother has left clear instructions for the service; not the tone-deaf prose of the new religion but the King James Bible and Cranmer's Common Prayer, and the Nunc Dimittis: *Lord lettest now thy servant depart in peace.* As though party to her instructions, I have written Coward's lyrics on the white and yellow posy on her coffin: *I'll see you again.* On a shivery April day Canon Kirton, having travelled from Surrey to take the service at the family's request, waits at the church door to receive me on my father's arm just as he did on my wedding-day. Whether he detects the heavy musk of sherry beneath the spearmint on my breath I can't tell; I smile and smile so successfully that one of my Plumb aunts says afterwards how wonderfully I bore up. I smile again, as the room holding its last and fullest gathering of my family empties, as Canon Kirton waits to take his leave.

Can't you stay a little longer, I say, and he smiles and shakes his head and explains about the trains, and takes my hand and holds it for a moment.

God bless, he says; and he is gone.

The house cools, but the house is full. Full of my mother's books, her sewing, the scarves she wore against her neuralgia, a wardrode of Wilford Players' costumes; a smaller wardrobe of my mother's clothes I think at first that I might wear, but when I put my hand into the soft press of coats and dresses to choose something I change my mind and the Salvation Army is summoned to remove them in my absence. Her paints, her paintings, a white smock and a slender folding easel, a half-finished embroidery of a Bailey coat of arms she sent away for. Her jewellery, two scrapbooks, one for the WI, one the Wilford Players. Her piano, its piano-stool packed tight with sheet music: Chopin's *Nocturnes*, *The Desert Prince*, *Lilac Time*, *All in the April Evening*, the only duet we ever sang together. Her books: the crime novels, the evocations of the England of her youth: *In Search of England, A Shropshire Lad, The Parish Chest*. Her poets: Shakespeare, Browning, Kipling, Housman, the World War II poems of John Pudney, a commonplace book with her favourites written out by hand. No sign of the history of Wilford that she was writing, but I do not have the energy to search further for it now. I box the books in the old green metal trunk, and take a few of them home across the road, but no more than the novels are my mother's poets my poets, and in my childish rush to write I have never taken time to find any of my own.

199

Some things can not be put away. In the brown envelope, tucked behind the note my mother left me, there is another piece of paper, a folded newspaper cutting from The Observer headlined *Sir Douglas and Friend*. The friend in question is the late golf commentator Henry Longhurst, Douglas Bader's longtime golf and drinking companion. During Longhurst's last struggle with cancer, the two friends pondered the likelihood of an afterlife from the perspective of a shared agnosticism. As he drained his glass of gin, Longhurst promised Bader that he would let him know whether the grass was greener on the other side. A few months after Longhurst's death Bader was on his way to a function when he was approached by a medium who said that she had a message for him from someone called Henry. She was to tell Bader that the grass was greener.

The newspaper account seems to have appeared in January, when my mother was still alive; but like Bader, she has waited until her death to pass it to me, left the telling to someone's else's words, left their significance to silence. Perhaps her intention is only to offer comfort once again, comfort that can embrace both a godfearing mother and a godless daughter. But there are too many half-told stories in this story, too many things other than comfort: my mother's religion, her many selves: Laura, Ethel, Elvira; the older self I see only in monochrome, the girl with her scarf at the sea's edge.

And I am not comforted. I am fifteen again, back in my place in the audience of *Blithe Spirit*, perched on a

200

wooden chair in the front row of the church hall. Only this time it is the end of the play: Elvira, already insubstantial, has slipped out into the wings, her words fading as she is banished to the spirit world. Alone on stage, with her wild and charmless hair and her glassy beads against her tweed, is Madame Arcati, the medium, holding the drawn curtains closed behind her. She is standing sentinel, her séance done, yet not confident; keeping on looking round, as if hearing whispers at her back.

*There are more things in heaven and earth,* she says.

She is a stranger, not speaking to me, yet with a look of the hypnotist in the set of her mouth; her message floating in the air between us, never quite coming to earth. The play runs to its end without cast or audience; the sceptical writer is driven from the home still haunted by his wives, while vases crash to the floor and *Always* plays endlessly on the gramophone.

I try to rise from my seat, but my legs are dream-legs made of iron. I pull myself up, get to the back of the hall, open the heavy doors and stumble down the steps. The doors crash to behind me and the hall fades out into the night. Outside, the night smells of ink, is dark as ink. No twinkling chimneys in the sky, no streetlights on the avenue where I have lived all my life. Just blackout.

## 15

## *North*

I do not go to pieces straight away. There is a lull before my collapse, a time when my mother's grave is just a turfed mound in the churchyard, before the lead text is hammered into stone. During the lull, my understanding of what has happened goes into a kind of suspension only interrupted by bouts of panic; the reflexes of a physiology which bypasses my conscious brain and throws me into cycles of breathlessness and pounding heart. The doctor assesses the tremor in my shaking hands and prescribes Ativan, a new generation tranquillizer which, for most situations, damps down my nervous system as effectively as morphine damps down pain, and is equally addictive. Like any addict, I keep my drug beside me at all times, the sheets of silver foil punched with their reassuring blisters of blue pills. At night I sleep dreamlessly. In the daytime the world drifts by, blurred as the countryside from the window of a train.

Until one day in May, when we are driving up the motorway on a visit to my in-laws and the pulsing lights and wave of orange cones of a major roadworks nudge us into a stretch of contraflow. As we head north on the southbound carriageway the panic rises. I want to stop, I say, but the hard shoulder is beyond the crash barrier in a no man's land of steaming tarmac and rubble roads with their surfaces peeled away and we cannot stop. We roll down windows but the rush of accelerated air and cars is too much like the static in my head, and they are closed again. Shut in the hurtling car the panic surges like a geyser and I am screaming *Let me out* with both hands on the door-handle. Ahead a gap in the barrier and a temporary sign, *Services*; Shall I, asks my husband, and, Yes, yes, I say, and we swerve left and stop on a flat grey prairie of car park, my heart hiccupping sporadically as it slows to normality, a scum of cold tea in the polystyrene in my hand.

We limp home and she is not there. Not on the end of the phone, not across the road, sitting quiet at her sewing with the TV closed down. She is out in the open, under molehills of damp soil in the graveyard. I stand there with the rows of graves around me like grey shoots of a dead spring and put my flowers in the punctured vase. I face forward, across the river, to where the power station chimneys used to be. Nothing left now of the old brick chimney but the hollow finger of a stubborn stump left at its base; not even that, of the concrete chimney that kept the black snow from the church and threw it high into the sky. Just a brief impression of their shape, faint plumes of white smoke dispersing on the wind.

I face forward. Grave, river, the pink brick slab of the power station, skeletons of pylons. Behind me, the stretch and curve of Wilford: church, trackless railway, hogweed seeding in the Willowwoods, the bike freewheeling on the footpath, the man in sunglasses leaning on the riverbank railings watching me. Madame Arcati, talking in my head, her script still running.

I cannot look round. Where I was once rooted, beneath my feet, the ground shakes as with the aftershock of detonation, rippling like a shockwave across the river. I turn from the grave and go, my old life diminishing at my back.


So, says the therapist, you're moving away.

Yes, I say.

She looks at my notes.

The Lake District. That's quite a move. Do you have family or friends there? I shake my head.

Well, I hope it works out for you, she says.

She closes the file and looks up. I smile and thank her for her time. Then I am out of the building, jumping from the steps into the splash of sunlight on Regent Street. Running already, my heart in my throat, rounding the corner before she can call me back.

We know nobody in Cumbria. Only, by proxy, the writer of the seven walking guides whose lyric text prescribes its mountains as a place of rest: from grief, from anxiety, from people; a text that bolsters my lifetime's instinct when in distress to flee from people, not to some empty night but to wild places, mountains that Wainwright has built with his pen on the page, long walks on firm rock and grass to the grey cones of summits which will put the bone back into the day. We will, as he did, move into this fairyland and fuse ourselves to its beauty.

Our houses, whose proceeds we will pool to buy a single house in the Lakes, sell quickly. Almost as quickly we find our dream home in Keswick: a substantial stone house whose south-faced back rooms look straight down Borrowdale to the fort of boulders marking England's highest point. From our bedroom the view drops down in perfect landscape composition: a crested wave of mountain, low wooded hills, the shifting horizontal of the lake. Pickfords' navy lorries come and go and we are ensconced, sharing a kitchen with my father but otherwise autonomous, free to align ourselves with the artistic tradition of the district: my husband making the bespoke furniture he has always dreamed of doing, while I will write again as soon as I am fully recovered. In the meantime, there is walking. All winter the mountains are high white over vivid cerulean lakes; in summer we walk at dawn and dusk, our boots end-stopping the lean shadows that stretch out behind us, while at midday the heat boils off into the mountains and melts their rock into a heather haze. The older, peopled world of home flickers occasionally through in TV news reports: the flare of braziers and truncheons and convoys of shrouded coal-lorries as, once and finally, Margaret Thatcher breaks the miners.

In Keswick I skirt the populated world where possible, leaving folded requests at surgeries for my tablets, asking my father to collect my Courvoisier during his daily shop. Mostly we are left alone. There is a Cumbrian word for strangers in the district: 'offcomers,' who, it is said, stay seven years and then are gone. In Keswick the offcomers are the literate class, huddling together in writers' groups in the lounges of the more formal hotels; the real Cumbrians, on-foot farmers and hunters on the fells, ignore them and wait for them to leave. We take our daytime walks unwelcomed, our imminent departure written into the culture.

The panic hits in the evenings, driving me from the house into the shaded garden spotted with the dayglo colours of mesembryanthemums, down to the fence and back, anything as long as I am moving. I am on a bottle of brandy a week, a numbing supplement for the blue pills whose steady dose I never exceed; the ways of psychiatrists far too well known to me for any confession of how bad the black times are. Neither my husband nor my father can reconcile my twin selves of intrepid walker and nervous wreck. Even to myself I have become a baffling contradiction: scaling the cairns of Pike O' Blisco with the rain pitting my face like blown sand; curled like a snail beside the garage door, wailing for help. My husband and father look on helplessly, unable to guess which side will prevail.

I curl up; I keep curling. But I uncurl, and climb again, each time with a triangle of granite in my pocket, my stone to add to the grey cairn in the clouds. The thin air of altitude suits me, the distant view of soft cloud-blanket folded thickly over the streets below. Up on the tops I take to ridge-walking, stringing summits together without the need for descent. The topography seems an extension of the oscillation in my brain, reshaping any latent flat Midland thought into a mountain-shaped landscape of peak and trough. The peaks, as Wainwright has said before me, are both real and a metaphor for life, drawing an absolute distinction between those who fail to reach the summits, and the determined who will make it to the top.

Wainwright does not concern himself further with the fate of the failures. I imagine his weaklings as transplanted versions of my snail self, frozen to a crevice on Striding Edge as the determined stalk past them with lofty contempt. In this scheme of things, the weak and strong are separate strains of humanity; there is no place for their co-existence under the same skin. I itch to prove him wrong, but not by thrusting myself into the spotlight of example. My own skin feels too thin, too imperfectly stitched together, too prone to tear under pressure. Instead I begin the old search for an alternative skin, for a character who wears both fragility and strength on the outside as Alex did, whose physical presence will mirror the self beneath. I observe the population of the fells with care. Mostly those who venture onto the mountains are other walkers, humpbacked with haversacks, sweating and gasping upwards, but one bronze evening on the Fairfield Horseshoe there is a stick-thin fellrunner in singlet and shorts, skipping towards us on a steep descent, scree-slopes bubbling like waves beneath his feet; every step a potential fracture of racehorse legs. A roll of pebbles and he is past, a frail silhouette against the sun-blaze over Windermere. I hold my breath and watch, storing the shape of him in my head until he is out of sight.

The next time I see him he has a name.

The TV has absorbed my shift of thought and swept the miners from its schedules in favour of the build-up to the 1984 Olympics, taking place across the pond in a searing hot LA. Somewhere in the bright team parade beneath a jet-packed silver spaceman is middle-distance runner Sebastian Coe, bemedalled already from the last Olympiad, but with a point to prove. For two years the holder of world records has won no major title, bowing out of championships with injuries and undefined viral complaints. Four years after Moscow, he scores silver again at his strongest distance; but when tasked with this apparent failure he is cool and reticent, somehow holding his fallibility and potential in suspension. His duality goes over the heads of the Press pack, who close in on the dimension of defeat and, not waiting for the 1500 metres, pronounce Coe washed up, the elegant gazelle outpaced by the rangy Cruz. As the heats of the 1500 take place under a blistering sun, and Steve Ovett falls exhausted to the steaming track, no one, least of all England, expects much more of Coe.

I do not stay up to watch the 1500 final, hunkering down under the bedclothes with crossed fingers pressed against my cheek, but as the Cumbrian day breaks a few hours later I already know that he has won. It is a little later before the replay delivers the iconic image of a young man with set teeth and right arm raised, one finger pointing upward in a gesture to the press which does not have the crudity of a Higgins but the grace and nobility of a Tenzing: *Look, I have come through.* This is the second skin I need: gold, glowing, a victory played out at the moment when I need it most. Euphoria froths in my gut like penicillin.

I start to write again, shedding drugs and alcohol and weight as my confidence returns, naming the protagonist of my new novel Sebastian in honour of his inspiration. The narrative I plan will be a Victorian novel, in the traditional three volumes, set in the Derbyshire countryside of my childhood, the hollow green hillsides of a lead-mining region. My Sebastian will be a child, named after the image in his mother's painting of the saint, thrust into premature adulthood by her desertion. A child abandoned by a city-bred mother who cannot endure the twin silences of a Peakland farm and a taciturn husband, who leaves her son to face a deputation of lead-miners, their torches burning holes in the darkness of the farmyard, while his father wanders grief-struck through the fields. Sebastian will survive her betrayal, but at a cost. As he matures it will be as if something has receded in him, fading out the colour in his skin to the whiteness of limestone, so that his analogy in art shifts from painting to marble statue: smooth, perfect, hard.

But no hearts will be worn on sleeves in this novel. Women have returned to my fiction, but the reckless emotions of my medieval heroines are centuries away. Feelings have become subterranean, their pulses pinging in the dark like the stone Sebastian drops into the mineshaft. Left alone together, son and bereft father speak to one another in short, staccato sentences, the taut silences between them full of the wife and mother whose name is cut from conversation as if she were dead, not just hidden by the smoke-pall of the city where she has gone to lose herself. With her gone, an existential loneliness permeates the novel, a loneliness passed from my writing hand to Sebastian, until he is so heavily weighed down with unhappiness that, if we met in the mountains again, we would find that we had changed places; he, burdened and struggling; me, skipping the mountains with a light step.

Days pass, weeks, months, before this displacement is tested. I write my novel into thick lined slabs of A4 paper, sitting at the table in the bay window of our living-room, while in the garage my husband planes discarded timber into smoothness. Sometimes I glance out at the garden and the abrupt wooded slope of Walla Crag, but mostly I look so intensely down at my writing that when I shut my eyes I see the oblong of the page thrown into negative on my eyelids. Neither of us makes any money, and both of us look away from the financial support that must come, inevitably, from my father. Each month-end I suffer the disturbance of his ritual knock at our living-room door, his hand curling into the room holding the banknotes which are our monthly allowance, placing them carefully on the end of the sideboard.

Thankyou, I say.

My pen stops. My father is still in the room. I can feel him waiting, slightly stooped, in the doorway. The stiffness of his neck seems to transfer to mine. I write on, trying to finish my sentence.

I need to have a word, he says.

I put the pen down. I turn round.

My father is content in Cumbria. He has said so, many times, and for months now his only complaint has been that Keswick town is in the bowl of the valley, at the bottom of the hill on which our house stands; a hill he has to climb each day after the shopping trips that shape his daily life. But he is tired of the climb, tired of the weight of the bags that often hold no more than a tin of soup. He sits on the sofa with his arms spread out along its back and tells us that he cannot settle in the Lakes, that he has taken the decision to move back to Nottingham. He does not ask us what we think, he does not ask if we have considered our own plans. I nod and take the news calmly while my husband, who knows that we cannot afford to run the house alone, weeps.

When my father has gone back to his room I pick up the money from the sideboard. It is as light as air.

The night after we have taxied my father and his cases to Penrith Station I drink a half-bottle of his parting gift while my husband sleeps beside me on the sofa. As I drink I can hear my ears singing. A familiar sound, not the wave-rush of panic but the sound that whistles in my blocked ears when I come down from a summit too quickly, the deafness that reminds me that in two years I have not fully acclimatized to the hills. At 3 a.m., without warning, my ears unblock. In the room shapes seem suddenly to resolve themselves: the dark oblongs of windows, the pillar of the dim standard lamp; my husband, sunk in the valley of the sofa. In front of me, the closed-down TV, a faint grey reflection of my head and shoulders on its screen. Pictures flash in my brain and disappear: Sebastian, hanging over the cold air of the mineshaft, listening for the stone hitting bottom; Sebastian, calling in vain for his father, watching the lights advancing up the lane.

In the darkness I find the phone, pick it up and dial. When I hear the one-word answer I stiffen, and for a moment Sebastian's stoicism buttresses my voice.

No. It doesn't matter.

Yes, it does, a female voice says. Don't ring off.

He's gone, I say, sobbing openly down the phone. My father. He's walked out on us.

The disembodied voice - a therapist, perhaps, or merely someone who has volunteered to answer the phone - encourages me to talk. I say my piece over and over again, but with each repetition the loneliness increases. I can hear my own words going out into space, fading down the line into the black rural night. After a while I put the phone down. At last I sleep, dreaming of the lead-miners breaking down the gate, torching Sebastian's farm into a beacon. And Sebastian, standing at the gate as they finally retreat, saying They'll never go.

In the morning the first thing I see is my pen, lying aslant across the white pad on the table. Sebastian is still there on the page, immobile by the farm gate, trying to summon the strength to move. After the trailed last sentence of the chapter, there is a blank half-page, and a horizontal line marking the end of the first volume. Beyond that line is the unwritten second volume, and the story of Sebastian's hard journey into adulthood, a story I know I cannot write in this room. The light is back in the windows, the mountains curtain the sky, but the flight to the north is over. It is time to go home.

## *16*

## *Southern*

I am driving alone to work along the north bank of the Trent. It's a strange thing, this aloneness, this sole responsibility for the car; I'm not used to it yet. Not used to my hands on the hard texture of the steering wheel, to the delicate shifts that turn the whole car on the road; not used to the stopping and starting that follows the lean of my feet on the pedals. And especially not used to the empty place beside me where I used to sit, the seat that still seems to bear the impress of a person in the hollow of its back, the dint in the headrest: not my shape, or my husband's, or my father's, just a shape, but someone else. It's a seat I could still re-occupy if I weakened and let my husband drive me to work. But for now, at least, I am strong.

*Keep left*, the road-signs say. Or they used to, years ago; now I am a driver I realize they don't say much at all but signal silently in pictures, like semaphore for the deaf. A white arrow on a blue ground points me left, away from the strip of tarmac in the no-man's land beyond the dashed white line where the cars rush towards you coming the other way. Keep left, away from the no man's land, the rushing cars, the verge beyond them, the dark grey river beyond the verge that glints in the right periphery of my vision, the south bank across the river. Away from the right-field glimpses of Wilford

Church and the Ferry fields and the smooth green span of the new Toll Bridge stretched tight across the water.

Another sign. 20, in a red circle. Slow down, not for children or horses or other cars because none of these are visible today on the Embankment. But slow, so that the Embankment road unfurls in even slower motion, keeping to its side of the river, turning to the left as the river bends back on itself, as the north bank pushes out into its own isthmus and the south bank retreats into the soft concave sweep of the Willowwoods. Slow, so that the Willowwoods on the far side of the river pass almost at walking pace: deserted, no children, no fishermen, the old paths gone to couch and thistle and hogweed, the riverside willows grown tall and broad, their trailing branches fishing the fast dark current. Trees colonizing the disused railway embankment, its bridge hacked away, just a girdle of blue brick left around the stump of earthwork that stops fifty yards short of the water.

The car judders and the needle on the rev counter drops. I put my foot down and change up into third. On my side of the river the trees are neatly trimmed, the roadside verges open out into a wide plain of sports field. Beyond the field the Meadows rise up in a wall of council housing, one half new, one old. On the left, the demolished and rebuilt half, where old roads are thinned to walkways and new dead-end closes twist back and forth around lean houses with slit windows and stockade fences. On the right, the half that escaped the bulldozers, an inner core of die-straight streets and neat terraced houses. I contour the sports field and turn off the Embankment into a tree-lined street leading to the centre of the core. Riding the nib-sharp junction of Wilford Grove and Wilford Crescent is the Meadows Library, a wedge of building styled like a Nonconformist chapel or a synagogue, its imposing entrance sheltered by a slate-grey cupola and sandstone columns, its walls winging outwards to fill the space between the streets. I park the car and let myself in with my key at the back door, turn the lights on and, humming Billy Joel's *Uptown Girl* to myself, start sorting out the issue desk.

On the north side of the river, where we have settled since coming back to Nottingham, I feel as if I can start anew. One of the first things I do on our return is book an appointment with an optician for a contact lens consultation. I know that this time I will succeed, just as clearly as I knew, at seventeen, that I would fail. It is as if the old life was a negative of the new; now, everything is reversed. Even this battered suburb feels new land to me, *new land* like the legends on the old explorers' maps, the words stretching out to fill the white uncharted space, and I attempt to make myself equal to its newness with my car and my new contact lenses, learning to drive on streets that do not dwindle to bridges but cross and meet one another in comfortable patchwork; looking wide-eyed into the staffroom mirror, my vision twenty-twenty through the membrane of the soft lenses that sit gently on my eyes, a generation beyond the hard glass discs my mother wore. In the mirror I see a thing I have never seen since my childhood: a focused, unencumbered reflection of my face, my eyes peeled of glasses, bright as new skin. I leave the staffroom, the edges of my world sharp and clear, and make for the double front doors, ready to admit the public.

Most days it is work that my friend Jessica and I could do with our eyes shut. To stave off boredom we lean against the counter, comparing broken nails and passing comments on the borrowers and the idleness of our colleagues. Jessica has a blonde shaggy perm, and an armful of silver bracelets that clatter as she delves into the issue; she drives her black Fiesta with bare feet and reverses it into impossible spaces. Together, both women in our thirties, we are girls again: we shop for clothes, drink bad wine at the Meadows' street-corner pubs, revel in the jewellery and makeup that create the selves we wish to be: able, confident, the antithesis of library ladies. We laugh a lot, occupying the here and now like a personal fortress: Jessica talks of job offers and her boys, now old enough to be left while she goes out to work, I talk of my novel. I start to talk fast, picking up the patterns of Jessica's speech. It feels like tap-dancing, with only our toes touching the floor. We are at the beginning of things, both of us. It is an unspoken article of faith.

When I work without Jessica the energy falters. My other colleagues do their work in as leisurely a fashion as Jessica is urgent, reading novels on the counter, gazing dreamily downwards as the borrowers cough for attention and hand their books to me, knowing I will pass them through my hands unread, date-stamping them and pushing them back across the counter. But one quiet Friday I find myself with a spare hour in the staffroom and a book on the table that someone has left behind, a Local Studies production of anecdotes, old photographs and poetry about the good old days of the Meadows. There are school groups, black-faced colliers, horse-drawn milk-floats and vistas of long straight streets misting into infinity. Photographs of the 1947 floods, the Trent levelled to a lake, spilling its excess out across the plain: both Ferry fields and Willowwoods submerged, only the Toll Bridge standing proud of the water. As I skim the accompanying text, the images rise from the page like flotsam. The last slim chapter chronicles the 1970s demolition of the Meadows, and here the text peters out. Half a dozen photographs: a man in working clothes and his bashful, thumb-sucking daughter pose smiling on the scoured patch of ground where their house once stood. An old lady with a shopping bag and fur-lined ankle boots stands on another patch of blitzed ground, her head turned away from the shell of the church where she was organist. An aerial view of the demolished suburb: not only buildings but the patterns of the streets rubbed out, scribbled over with the tyre-treads of bulldozers, marking out the curves that will become the amnesiac closes of the new Meadows, lost, leading nowhere. A few traces of black oblongs on the ground where terraces of houses stood.

All gone.

I shut the book and go back into the library. My colleague is staring into space.

You might as well get off, I say. Jessica's on at half past.

She gives me a hazy look.

All right, dear.

As Jessica comes down the steps she says:

Have you made your mind up yet?

Not yet, I say.

There is a vacancy at the library. Not a temporary job like the one I hold at present, but a permanent post, that will yoke Jessica and I together in what might be years of comfortable friendship. Since going back to work, my life seems to have settled into a kind of balance, my existence divided into two parts, equally weighted, that never touch. At home, I live my inner life of writing, telling the story of my Sebastian's life in private: he suffers and endures, the reins of business firmly in his hands, his debts pressing harder on his thin shoulders. After each shift of writing I go placid to bed and fold myself into dreamless sleep, waking fresh to my daytime shifts at the library, ready for the smalltalk of everyday life. There is depth and surface. Each has, and knows, its place.

But something in the prospect of permanence has disturbed this balance. There is a contract on the staffroom table, one Jessica has brought in for me to look over. Provisions and conditions and a white space at the end for the employee's signature. When I go to bed I am no longer placid; asleep, I dream of contracts. Sometimes they are maps with *New Land* written across them; sometimes only contracts with the dotted line and white space for my name at the foot of the page. I dream of Jessica handing me the pen to sign, of my hand shaking, hovered over the space, unable to form the letters of my name. Finally I lower the pen to the page and see that there are other marks, indentations, on the paper: the ghosts of signatures that have gone before me. I can't sign this, I say, and she stands over me, arm folded over silver arm, asking What's the problem?

I can't explain.

The afternoon wears on. The last of the schools depart and the windows turn blue in the dusk. I look over at the entrance. After about six o'clock the local youths tend to congregate in the vestibule between inner and outer doors, laughing and joshing one another in Urdu, Punjabi and Gujerati. Mostly they are good-humoured, these new Meadows people with their black beards and dark turbans tight-wound into dimpled domes on their heads; but whenever I pass them I see, fast as a blink, an image from my schooldays: the daily gauntlet-run of Meadows boys, their Deering uniforms soot-dark, pouring over the Toll Bridge towards me as I tried to make my way home. Meadows boys who should be gone for ever along with their pulverized homes, dispersed on the brick-dust wind to the far corners of the city; but somehow here again, reconstituted, blown back in to their old haunts.

Tonight the vestibule is empty; but as I look someone comes in at the outer door. A young man, smart in Chinos and designer leather, *not from round here*, as the older borrowers would say. He looks round, and comes up to the counter.

Does Jessica still work here? he says.

She's in the Junior Library, I say. I'll get her.

Who shall I say? I ask.

He stands with his hands in his pockets. Easy, elegant, decidedly not from round here.

John, he says.

Jessica is on her hands and knees, shelving a trolley full of picture-books.

I feel like I've been down the pit, she says as I come in, shaking her bracelets up her arm. I'll have to scrub everything when I get home.

I tell her about the visitor. She looks up, through the glass screen toward the counter. John takes a hand from his pocket and raises it.

Can you hold the fort for a while, she says to me.

There is no sign of them when I go back to man the counter. The blue turns to dark, the doors swing and the vestibule fills up. The new Meadows boys spread across the entrance and get in the way of the few borrowers who come out in the evening. Mr Attercliffe slams his Zane Greys on the counter and tells me I should throw the buggers out. I'll help yer if yer like, he says. I smile and shake my head and look at the clock. Seven-twenty. I pick up the westerns and go round the counter to shelve them. Jessica and the young man are sitting talking beside a low table between the stacks. As I come into view the young man looks up at me and the conversation drops into a whisper. I turn my back and start to force my books into the tight wedged shelves. The books are grimed and sticky with the grease of many hands. Guns, lassos, tomahawks on their yellow spines.

I'll lock up, then, shall I, I say.

Thanks, says Jessica, passing me her keys.

# The Memory of Bridges

The air in the vestibule is pungent with spice and sweat. Excuse me, I say, getting hold of one of the oak doors, The library is closing now. The new Meadows boys laugh and a youth without a turban leans on the door. All right, sweetness, he says, and they laugh again. I take a step back and a turbaned boy who is leaning against the wall in front of the founder's dedication says Let the lady close up, Hardeep, and they start to file out into the evening. See you tomorrow, says Hardeep as he goes, and as I push the first door to I can hear the clear sound of the boys calling out one another's names in the street. Behind me, beyond the inner door propped open into the almost-empty library, the murmur of conversation, soft now, slower, like a mother reading a story to a child.

I move across to close the second door. To the left of the frame is the board of the founder's dedication, painted words sealed tight into varnished wood.

*The Southern Branch Library was opened by the Rt. Hon the Earl of Elgin and Kincardine, Chairman of the Carnegie United Kingdom Trust, on March 11th, 1925.*

Southern. It must be a mistake, I think, the dedication board rescued from a long-since demolished library. This is Meadows Library, Meadows as it says on the green perspex sign outside, as Jessica says when she rings me for a last-minute shift. *Southern* is a name that takes me back, back and back until I see myself ten years earlier, working at County Hall, packing cardboard boxes in the loading bay, packing them with old books that nobody wants to read any more. I see myself closing the flaps of the box and writing the destination with a black marker pen on the cardboard: *Store, Southern Library*. I see the porters take the boxes and slide them coffin-style onto the ribbed floor of the library van; see the van drive away, slow and weighted, and sunlight streaming into the loading bay. So many boxes, I say to my mother as we walk home along the riverbank, it must be one heck of a store. And she turns and says to me, her voice soft over the ticking wheels of the bike:

I used to work there, you know. During the war.

The memory starts to run like a river underneath my feet. I try to stop it, to hold myself in the present, in the here and now. No, this is Meadows, I want to say, I'll prove it to you. I pull the oak door wide open and go out into the street. There's the council sign beside the entrance, still where it was last time I looked: *Welcome to Meadows Library* picked out in black on a lime green ground. But the proof isn't good enough, my eyes aren't good enough, not in this light, not even through the prism of my lenses. I edge further backwards, first onto the street and then across the street, back until I'm far enough from the building to see the stone parapet rising above the cupola, a parapet with two lines of white stone letters carved into the fabric of the building. There's just light enough left to read them, light enough to be sure there's no mistake: *Nottingham Public Libraries. Southern Branch.*

*I used to work there. During the war.*

222

I stand still, teetering slightly, on the nib of the junction. This is where the van was going, where the books were going, to be taken into the shelter of its basement for the duration; while the old Meadows were pounded to dust until brick-red clouds hung round the building and the library stood like a church amidst the devastation, stronger than a church, holding its old name aloft like a spire.

And that other duration. The one I can't get back to, the five years of dark and bomb and searchlights panning for a target in the blackout streets where somewhere my mother, scarf knotted tightly, hurries home; where back in the empty library, her signature loops across the contract on the table. I feel the surface of the present peel away until there is only dark running depth, only layer upon layer of the past. I'm not treading new land where I can build from scratch, I'm not where I thought I was. I'm back in my former life, long ago, having one of my mother's surprises sprung on me.


That was a bit of a shock, says Jessica as I hand the keys back to her. I haven't seen him for years.

I look round but I can't see the young man. Can't see him but that doesn't mean he isn't there, out of sight between the stacks.

*I've had a bit of a shock myself.*

We thought we might make a go of it, years ago, she says. But it didn't happen.

Some things just don't work out, I say.

I follow her up the steps towards the staffroom. The contract is still on the table where I left it. Already I can see the faint outline of the new staff member who will fill the vacancy: a smiling Asian girl with no memory, who will come and go through the back door and never see the white stone letters, never hear the word Southern.

Can you turn the lights out, Jessica says.

I flick the switches one by one and, piece by piece, my mother's library vanishes: counter, chairs and tables, bookstacks, founder's board; the door I've never seen, leading down into the basement where the old books must still be resting in their boxes, still packed away.

We leave in the full dark, the inner spaces of our cars illuminating as we ease ourselves into them, one another's smudged silhouettes briefly visible in our rear-view mirrors. Behind me, the library and its two names vanish in the gloom, the shape of the empty seat beside me in my left-field vision as I drive away.

## *17*

## *The Ladder*

Back home my fictional Sebastian is waiting for me. As I walk into my study and throw the car keys on the table I can see him in the mirror behind me. He's dressed in a lead-miner's gear, ready to descend into the depths of the shaft. An old leather jacket belted round his thin waist, a broad-brimmed hat on his head, unlit candle ready in its band. His eyes are black, matt as soot. I don't want to pick up my pen and go down with him, down the iron ladder into the coffin-levels and the chamber down below where the miners chip away at ore, signing to one another above the pounding of the pumping-engine. I'm tired, I say, too tired to write. I shut the door on him and go to bed, keeping my eyes tight closed until it's light.

Summer comes and with it the athletics season. Light counterbalances the dark until in June the night seems driven away for ever but by July the days are already, imperceptibly, shrinking. I chase the light as long as I can, driving down to every meeting at Crystal Palace, where there is no palace but a green hill topped with a radio mast that winks its red eye at Concorde as she passes overhead on golden Friday evenings. Within the stadium, Coe floats light as air above the red stippled track; after his races he is cool, polite, posing willingly for photographs, and I ask calmly for his signature, volunteering no other conversation. There is no danger in these sunlit meetings, no whiff of the smoky air of snooker halls. Only once do I hear him talk out of turn in public, his light voice magnified by the interviewer's microphone, speaking out against the new system of Olympic trials that will deny him selection for the 1988 Games. There will be no third gold medal, no more victories pulled from defeat, no more trips to Crystal Palace. Coe's life, or *afterlife* – his own word for his retirement – will continue, but his athlete's race is run. I am in the stands for his swansong, an attempt to better his decade-old world record, bearing flowers that I never hand to him. The floodlights catch the lift of his arm as he rounds the final bend and waves farewell. Then he's gone.

And when I come home from that last meeting, go into my study and throw the car-keys on the table, it's in my head that his alter-ego will be gone too: that the mirror will be clear, rubbed clean of him. But my Sebastian is still there in the mirror, the unlit candle in his hat, waiting for me to write him down the ladder into the mine, to forge rungs that will be strong enough to hold him. But his eyes are blacker than they were last time I looked, tunnelling deep into his head into a place that feels beyond any words. And without them, I don't know how to light the candle. I don't know how to bring him up again.

For the second time in my life I turn to reading. Writers should read, so I was always told, but I never wanted to. My history books were different. Hard facts for me to soften and mould into my narrative. But not other people's novels, other than the ones I knew so well they had lost their power to reshape my thoughts, the ones I read each night like prayers, for the comfort of repetition. Now I'm turned away from my own novel other people's fiction feels like a new place to hide, a place where I can rest from the intensity of Sebastian's world, from the intensity of isolation itself. The loneliness has got to me. I find myself longing for the old, gathered-in sense of community; not gathered around one of the failed centrifuges of family and church but around the world of learning, where even reading, the most solitary of occupations, can be socialized. I join an Adult Education class in Victorian literature, taught by a young woman whose brown spiral locks and unruly eyebrows resemble mine. Our tutor does not sit behind the desk but perches on top of it, mistress of her subject and easy with her students. I don't precisely think, this is how I will do it when I teach, but I feel the twinge of a possible future.

This social reading might have sent me back to my novel, ready to marshal Sebastian's life into shape, but it doesn't happen. Reading is the first stage in the process of analysis, and it is analysis that she calls for: of character, of the author's intentions. *Read between the lines*, she says, a thing that is second nature to me, a skill I have been honing all my life. In a chilly classroom at Shakespeare Street we sit in judgment on Dickens and Thackeray and Mary Ann Evans, approving one another's insights, ears constantly pricked for our tutor's praise. Our criticism feels a powerful thing. More powerful than the books themselves.

And the more I exercise this new skill, the more it becomes the future. On the eve of the new decade, I receive a letter telling me that, at my third attempt – the first two were half my life ago – I have been admitted to the University of Nottingham to study English, and in September 1990 I pass beneath a colonnade into a quad enclosed by a square of marble buildings, each white wall pierced with rows of tall sashed windows. A Christminster, if ever there was one; but I have no intention of playing Jude. Behind each window I know there is an office lined with books, a seminar, a group I am now authorized to join. My subconscious, grown into a dark troubling mass behind my eyes, shrinks slowly out of sight. The conscious – clever, knowing, its hand perpetually in the air with the right answer - moves into the vacated space.

For a while I tell people at university that I have written novels, but the raised eyebrows and half-smiles soon silence me, and from silence I pass into a state of embarrassment, suddenly doubtful about the merit of my efforts. Soon we have all read Roland Barthes' *Death of the Author*, and discovered that a writer is not a godlike being but a collection of socially conditioned responses, that the author's intentions and experience are of no importance; only the critical reading has significance. I think of my historical novels, shelved behind the glass of the china cabinet at home, their spines on show to the world, their lurid bookjackets squeezed tight together out of sight. I try to remember the words I wrote, but the print is hidden in a press of paper where only the white edges show. Other words are jostling for space in my mind, new books appearing, barging my novels to the back of the cabinet: shiny textbooks with no pictures on their covers, their pages heavy with dense dark print. My own books crouch in their shadow. Slowly, I forget them.

During my first year I read the new books assiduously, thrilled to be a student at last, enjoying the community of other matures: a retired police inspector, a working-class Scouser with a dry wit, a wiry lady whose off-campus relaxation is climbing. In a spirit of cheerful mischief I submit right-wing essays for my Marxist lecturer, and a paganist reading of Old English poetry for my staunchly Christian professor. My essays come back with high marks and approving comments, comments I hug to myself like a blanket. I am caught by Father Brown's invisible line, ready to be reeled in again and again. Or perhaps not Father Brown, not a text so simplistic, so parochial. Something later, colder, more clinical.

But as my second year progresses, I begin to enjoy the dismemberment of beloved books a little less, and I opt not for the abrasive atmosphere of Critical Theory, but for Medieval Studies. Classes are small, quiet, select, the atmosphere of the scriptorium. Our task is translation, to render the Old and Middle English originals into lucid modern English. I enjoy the displacement of time, the removal from the battlefield of theory, the faintly acknowledged memory of a place

230

where I felt safe. If no longer Catherine, still I can fancy myself a scribe, my umber hood dropped over my head, my face in shadow, my voice intoning the correct translation word by word.

Yet even in Medieval Studies I am caught on the cusp of the need for approval. Now if I don't understand my text I do not ask for help but trawl the library until I find an old translation I can paraphrase. Mistakes are for my peers. *forði him luueden God and gode men*: not 'therefore he loved God and good men', as the other students have rendered it, but 'God and good men loved him'. Splendid, says my tutor, you've understood that construction. I have the grace to look downward at my page as the others correct their work. At the year-end I learn my translations by heart and reproduce them in exams in the vast dark-curtained space of the Sports Centre.

The final year of my degree comes and with it a question I can't answer. What the afterlife is going to be, what happens after graduation. University work has spread morning, noon and night into my life, sweeping my unfinished novel into a drawer, papering its way through the back bedroom and evicting the spare bed to clear space for desks and cupboards. It is generally agreed that I have spread and grown, found the niche kept empty for me through my years of failure; not a place where my mother has preceded me but the blank white space of *new land* at last. Not quite blank, as it will be shaped by the conventions of the higher degrees: first a master's, then a PhD. But within these conventions, I can forge my own enquiring path.

*The Memory of Bridges*

My waking self accepts this reasoning. But at night my subconscious takes my academic surroundings and twists them into shapes that are not new but the half-familiar, shifted landmarks of dreams. Every day I pass the tall slim chimney of the university's heating system, a chimney so high that on sunny days its shadow stretches back down the campus road towards the north gate, and on foggy days its tapering black tip disappears into the mist. During my third year I start to experience a recurring dream: I am climbing the metal ladder that runs to the chimney's top, climbing so high there's no way down. When I glance over my shoulder I see a forest of other chimneys far below me; short truncated stumps of broken chimneys from the old power station, a twist of smoke issuing from each ragged mouth.

I freeze to the ladder. There is a sensation of falling, but it's the chimney falling, swaying in the thin air, shuddering over the hollow of its foundations, and if I don't get down it will take me with it. As I start to descend, the chimney vanishes; and suddenly I'm at the top of a children's slide on the Embankment with a queue of Meadows kids behind me. I'm weeping and clinging to the handrails, tucking my feet under me, backing away from the polished chute, shouting *I want to get down*. But no sound, no words, come from my mouth, only smoke. I wake up, my heart drumming, and lie there waiting for the sky to pale to grey, for the drumming to fade to background noise.

In July I pose for the obligatory graduation photograph, flanked by my husband and my father. There is pride in my husband's eyes, delight in my

232

father's: his mouth slightly open, ready to broadcast the news that his daughter is no longer a nervous wreck but top of the class again; that she is, after all, the clever girl he thought she was all those years ago, when she rode the lift to his skyscraper office to report her 'A' level results.

Between them I stand in the official pose, my hands either end of the blank sheet of card rolled and ribboned to simulate a certificate, the froth of my eighties perm escaping from the tight band of my mortarboard. A smile seems to be working its way down my face, a smile my mouth can't quite complete. My mouth is slightly twisted, embarrassed, lips pressed shut. Too self-conscious, in that moment of triumph, to speak.

The research years begin. The scaffolding of taught and timetabled modules falls away and my days are my own to organize. Shapeless days, padding back and forth between my monk's cell in the Graduate School and the campus library, where the cold blast of the airconditioning is a directionless wind blowing endlessly from invisible grilles. On the library's lowest floor are the books I need to study: great slabs of volumes of Anglo-Saxon poetry, facsimiles of texts whose precious originals are safe under lock and key at Cambridge. Facsimiles or not, they must be placed on silk cushions, their pages weighted with strings of lead beads sheathed in velvet; pencils handed out to scholars who wish to study them. At the end of a year my notebooks are full of these soft grey words, pale as ink faded under sunlight.

But it's not just the pencil that gives my notes their fugitive quality. Something is going wrong with the mechanics of my writing. My hand is tightening around the pen, my index finger curling back into the crook of my thumb, disassociating itself from the task. Within the notebooks my letter-forms sink to a weary ripple on the lines of the page, while increasingly my writing hand struggles to shape them, clenching to a frozen grip around the pen. The doctor diagnoses Writer's Cramp, a focal dystonia common, he says without irony, in those who have done a great deal of writing. There is no treatment, but, by the 1990s, the computer has become a ready alternative to the pen, and each carrel in the Graduate School is furnished with its own PC. I take thankfully to the change, to the quiet keyboard and the flashing cursor waiting for my words, but I rejoice especially in the invisibility of my mistakes. Throughout my undergraduate years I have used Granny Bailey's electric typewriter to write my essays, marking their pristine sheets with thick blotches of correction fluid to whiten the heavy indentations of misspelt words. On the PC screen the wrong words, the uncertain and halting words vanish without even leaving the ghost of liquid paper. My errors are smoothed away by processors whose workings I can't even imagine, slivers of artificial brains that shrink ever smaller year by year. The School hums with their industry, covering up the silence.

This is the long haul: no prizes, no marks, no flattering comments from my tutors but four, perhaps five years of study before the final graduation, but my father is still proud of me. Every Thursday, when I return home from university, he rings to ask how it's all going. I have little to report. There are things I could talk about but no longer have the words for: the emptiness of the library in the long vacation, the weariness of the endless translations of a dead language, the shake in my transcribing hand; the slow dawning that Medieval Studies is less escape than dead end. My brain seems to have altered its waves to the patterns of the computer, forgetting what it has deleted, the lost words on the screen transient objects that I can't retrieve. It's a long haul, I say, and I hear the customary nod as my father listens from his flat across the city, sitting in the old armchair that has travelled from Nottingham to the Lakes and back again. Not back to Wilford, though, not for either of us, bound by the tacit agreement that we can not go back; the vista from my father's elevated windows is not the old view of the railway bank but the fan of Nottingham's northern suburbs stretching away into a backlit sky.

Yet we have both made some kind of accommodation with the old life. Mine is to visit my mother's grave each month with flowers, dashing into the churchyard and out again before my emotions can catch up with me; my father's is a slower, longer walk back into the village and the sitting rooms of former neighbours. While I hold off, my father is drawn backward, into the house on Vernon Avenue we lived in but never owned; where an old friend, two decades widowed and living alone, is always happy to welcome him. Once, sometimes twice a week, he makes the old journey over the new Toll Bridge to visit the widow, to have tea with her in our old front room, to wander into the back kitchen with the pots and look out at the railway bank: so overgrown, he tells me on the phone, you'd never recognize it. As he talks I pull the spiral of the phone cord out straight and try to imagine the pale grass slope beyond the old garden fence, a bank no longer neatly mown but sprouting scrub and feral trees, excavating the ballast with their thick root systems, hanging their foliage over the old back garden. I try to imagine the top of the bank lost to sight, a scribble of branches across the clear straight horizon of the railway track. As I unclench my fingers from the phone cord I suddenly feel the sting of my fingernails burrowing into my flesh. There is a row of crescent pits in the palm of my left hand. And a painful sensation, like anger.

Two years pass. My thesis folders spread out across the shelves of a new bookcase. My father's friendship with his old friend progresses too, extending into more and more of his life. Their teas become days out, days out become holidays. The unspoken questions lodge in my mind. The old friend is not like my mother. She is not artistic, not literary, not musical. But my father has no need for these things: he likes his life as he has made it, level, even, comfortable. *I'm going to do nothing*, he said when he retired. I visualize them together, in the front room of my childhood home, tea set out on the table waiting for my visit. The two of them sitting silent and unoccupied, not so much like the ghosts of parents as the outer shells of their being. As if the trouble, the richness of an inner life which my mother and I shared never existed.

But my visit never happens. My father stops seeing the old friend, and I don't know why. Neither does my father, or so he says; only that they have fallen out, that there will be no more holidays, no more trips together, no more comfortable teas at number 30. My old home shrinks back behind my mind's eye. I'm glad to be done with the anger, with the visit I never wanted to make. But as the road to Wilford closes for a second time, my father's comfort is gone. Thrown back on his own resources, he resumes solo holidays, takes Sunday meals either with me or his one remaining sister. The heron's stoop appears again in his walk; there is less of him quite quickly, more bone in his face, more knuckle in his hands. He begins to talk about the future, about giving up his flat and going somewhere 'to be looked after'. When he says this, I know that he does not mean me; it is a euphemism for the word the old will not use. More than a euphemism, I will realize later, but not now.

We visit residential homes in his childhood suburb of West Bridgford. Dreadful places where my father's stoop is replicated and enhanced, where the old are left to shrink into the corners of their plastic chairs. One place is less pungent than the rest, within sight of the Cricket Ground but with a waiting list. We return home to reconsider; my father to his flat, me to my books.

Still every Thursday the phone rings. His voice has gone beyond nothing into plaintiveness. Mostly, when I ask, he is not feeling well but can't say how. He has a rash, fiery raw welts on his arms and legs that torment him at nights; his bedside cupboard is full of creams and salves and bottles calligraphed with Chinese characters. Visits to his doctor multiply, tests and finally a fact-finding stay in hospital. My husband and I follow with our questions, trawling the corridors for a specialist who went home hours ago. The nurse couldn't really say what the problem is, but hopes that he will be out in time for Christmas. A respite room awaits him at Rose Lodge on his discharge, but at the last moment he insists on going back to his flat. Within a week pneumonia has set in, a gasping, wordless forerunner of the last word he can't find breath to say; but a written word good enough for a cause of death, good enough for the signing-off of his death certificate.

I am called in to the hospital to say goodbye. His head is tilted back, his mouth open as if in the dentist's chair. Then he is quickly shrouded and gone, according to his wishes, his body given up to science. A fortnight later, on a cold February day, he is dust scattered into the thick grey air of the crematorium at Wilford Hill. No flowers, no grave, no headstone. I clear his flat and give his furniture to charity, deal with the solicitors. His number stays on the list beside my phone.

I return to university. Monday, Tuesday, Wednesday pass. I come home on Thursday and sit at my desk. I look at my pen laid slantways across my notebook, a fat pen with its plastic sheath cloaking the barrel to aid my grip. I look at the dark screen of my PC and listen to the silence. I shut my eyes and think of going to number 30 and knocking on the door, of my father's friend sitting in the front room, her back turned to the window, not answering. I think that I can hear a voice but it's the radio on, the words not quite audible. I stand at the door and call through the letterbox but I can't hear my words and I don't know what I'm calling. I bang the letterbox, watching as the slot of light flashes on the carpet. The doors are shut, front and back.

The doors are shut.

I open my eyes and look down at the book in front of me. Bede, *Historia Ecclesiastica*. The life of man is as a sparrow's flight through a lighted hall; from darkness into darkness. I think of Seb Coe running through the floodlight splash at Crystal Palace, rounding the final bend to wave farewell. Of the dark shuttering him from sight.

No grave, no memories, my father said in his note. No afterlife. Nothing left behind.

My husband knocks on the door and calls out to me.

Your dinner's been on the table half an hour, he says.

I shut the book and push it from me. At this moment, in *extremis*, I think suddenly of the hypnotist; of the old surgery where the brass nameplate once shone on the brick gatepost; where the nameplate is long gone, leaving a pale oblong, like a ghost of his passing, in the brick.

I need to talk to someone, I say.


The fifth week of counselling and the therapist and I are getting used to one another. We sit in a dimly lit room with a lamp on the table between us; a light that is nothing like the hypnotist's lava lamp with its red-orange globes, eternally rising and falling in their sticky liquid, but a steady lamp, its soft light glowing through a dull pink shade. This is university territory, but the walls surrounding us are lightweight, the roof roughly corrugated; it's a building with an ephemeral feel, one of a clutch of Nissen huts perched on the summit of the campus hill; around the buildings, the cherry trees that give them their name.

Slowly, gently, my therapist is helping me back down the ladder. Sometimes my ladder is the one running down the university chimney, sometimes it is the slide on the Victoria Embankment. Always, the direction is down. To clasp the rungs I must first unclench my hands from their writer's cramp, stretch the fingers out like wings. I am in therapy for grief, but once therapy has begun my grief spreads and spreads until it floods and flashbacks of my life float on its current: not just images of my father, trying to delete his existence with his last requests; but of my mother, ghosting the outline of her own life and death; of Canon Kirton's *God bless* as he turns away, the stumps of the old Toll Bridge, my head stretched back while the dentist takes away my teeth, the sea in my ears, the man leaning over the railings on the riverbank, the schoolfriends mimicking my fractured voice, the water pouring from the dramp, the flightless swan; my hand waving, waving to God on the guard's van of the train and him waving back.

As the flood recedes there's silence. I look out of the window. Outside grey horizontal dashes of snow fly past in the wind. Beyond the grainy prairie of the campus I can just see the clock on the white marble tower. Counting down the minutes until the end of my session.

Are you on the ground yet, the therapist says gently.

I test it with my feet. I can feel grass. Scuffed grass.

That's good, he says.

The clock winds up to strike the hour. The therapist shifts in his seat and suddenly I feel my voice rushing up my throat like a chased bird, flapping, panicking.

There's another ladder, I say.

He raises his eyebrows.

Sorry?

Another ladder. Down the mineshaft.

What mineshaft?

*The one in my —*

My chest heaves. He will throw me out, I'm five minutes over time. He doesn't throw me out. He waits. My chest heaves again and the bird flies out, scattering feathers around the room.

I say, I haven't always been an inmate of this Godforsaken place.

He looks at me.

No?

I say, *I used to be a writer.*

There's a pause.

Right, he says.

Another heave and the words come coughing out. The grief that couldn't speak its name, that can no longer even write its name, I tell him all about it. The quarter strikes and the therapist says,

Next time, we should talk about your writing. And we should talk about what's down there, at the bottom of this mineshaft.

I mop my eyes and nod. I want to say, It's been so long I don't know what's down there myself; but before the next session I dream of the ladder in my book. I watch Sebastian climbing down the iron rungs, I see him step off the ladder, the candle flickering in his hat. The walls of the limestone chamber shine like glass, giving his own face back to him and the tumbled rocks of the chamber, each reflection distorted but clear enough for his dilated, tunnelled eyes to see. Among the rocks, there are gravestones with no epitaphs, coffins with no nameplates; the missing names of those who are gone for ever, those who were real selves and bodies and those who were just words, like him, words that have vanished in the dark.

I put my hand on his arm. His rough sleeve is rolled to the elbow and the white forearm is wet with liquid ice. The stone is getting into his veins, turning him to marble. He can't stay here. I get behind him, my arms like crutches underneath his armpits, and push him back towards the ladder. Above us, a line of dripping rungs like dashes and a crack of light far up above; an uneven crack, a pale scrawl. Hard to say what's on the surface, beyond the light: old life, new life, afterlife.

I interlace my fingers with his, bend them to the rungs. We climb.

## 18

## *Dulce Domum*

There's cherry blossom sticking to my shoes. As I leave counselling, the PhD on pause for a year, I'm a writer again; but a convalescent writer, shaky, out of practice. I seek out a writing class where I can go incognito, with a lively tutor who lets me sink into the background when I want, picks on me when I need picking on. For the first time, I hear writers read their work aloud: sometimes with bravado, sometimes halting and stumbling as if their words were stones in their path. My words feel as if they will be the reverse: frail, inconsequential, specks of dust dispersing in the air.

The tutor finally picks on me to read at five to eleven on Remembrance Day. My story is ready, but it is long. My nameless heroine is embarking on a late marriage, looking forward to a life of calm companionship when a former lover comes to her flat and knocks on her door. The story opens as she turns, wondering whether to answer, as she walks slowly into her dark hallway, picking her way through the clutter of unopened boxes that have lain there since her move to a new home.

One of the class members looks up at the clock, and then at the tutor.

Aren't we observing? she says.

Oh, says the tutor, I think we'd rather have a story, wouldn't we?

The woman raises her eyebrows and leaves the classroom. I start to read - *Today, life begins* - and there is silence. I read through the distant strokes of Big Ben, through the two minutes' silence, through the cannon-burst salute. Around me the class is quiet. I think of black coats around the Cenotaph, parked trolleys in supermarket aisles; most of all, the woman sitting outside the classroom on the stairs, head down, hands clasped in front of her, observing. As I read I can see her through the glass panels of the door, head turned away, face hidden by a headscarf that is like my mother's. I read on. I feel as if I am doing something terrible, something exhilarating.

For now, the long haul of the novel, and Sebastian's fate, is in suspension, while I explore the short, the present day. Each time I finish a story, I seem to uncover another one beneath it. Closer, closer, to real life.


1999: my PhD creeps towards completion, and the news is full of the millennium bug. In the Graduate School nerves are frayed, and unofficial technicians gather round computers that, it turns out, were not built to cope with the number 2000. PhD students find a new source of income, prowling the carrels and pocketing undeclared fees for servicing and advice. Inside my own carrel, my Anglo-Saxon texts record the signs and portents of the first millennium: *In this year the moon was blood-red; In this year a great comet appeared in the sky.* A thousand years later, the tabloid headlines in the union shop leap from sign to prophecy: planes will fall from the sky, trains jump their tracks, missiles raise bullet heads from secret silos, while the computer systems which rule them go into meltdown.

But on a particularly dull May day, a human interest story ousts the doomwatch scenarios from the front pages of the tabloids: the parade of celebrities at the funeral of hellraiser Oliver Reed. Amid the press of black coats, there is a flash of white as a bony hand raises a blue Fedora in respect. Beside the lifted hand, the mourner's face is caught off-guard, startled, pale eyes turned sideways towards the camera. The headlines, more or less, are as one: *Hurricane Higgins dying from cancer.* Soon Higgins is being interviewed on TV, speaking out against the cigarettes that have scoured his throat and stripped his lower jaw of teeth. He scrapes the words from his throat: *Fucking fish and chip papers ... I'm not fucking dying ... I'm in remission.* His voice is sandpaper, his face working as it always did, his cheeks sucked away to nothing, his hair razored to fine tufts on his scalp. He is the weight of his skin, his bones and the suit hanging off them.

My old schoolfriend sends me an email.

I read he was dying, she says. I thought about you. I wondered how you felt.

I wonder, too.

May darkens to December. On the thirty-first the sky is quiet with so many planes grounded. Indoors, the TV crackles as Sydney fires a defiant blaze of fireworks into the year 2000; later the crackling is outside, sounding the sky like an echo chamber, tinting it mauve and gold into the small hours. We go out into the garden, the better to see a world not ending, but shooting stars of relief into the firmament.

*In this year there were many comets.*

In the late morning I brace myself and turn on my PC. The usual humming, and the monitor clicking static as it slowly comes to life, the date banded clearly across the foot of the screen: *1ˢᵗ January 2000.*

I sit down and start to write another story. Again a lover returns from the past, but this time the lover is dead, and the protagonist's existence revolves around the tending of his grave. One day, the lover comes back, and starts to talk to her. He talks and talks: *Back from death's door, I didn't die, you buried me alive* – he tries to talk her into speech, but she won't answer him. Her head is down, over the dead brown flowers in the vase, waiting him out until he accepts his death, until his voice wears out and she can have quiet again.

But he won't accept his death.

*You've kept me here against my will, he says, twisting round to look at the churchyard gate. I'm getting out of here.*

There's a sound of scuffling behind her as he turns to run. As his voice fades the woman finally raises her head to show her face. She is a young woman, an older woman, it's not clear. She's wearing glasses, the lenses fogged with tears or condensation, black winged frames that went out of fashion years ago. She kneels on the path, her knees wet with water from the vase, staring blind at the headstone, across the river, into the pale north sky. She hears the creak of the churchyard gate as

247

he makes his escape and she's up on her feet, her legs shaking because she's been crouching down there so long, twisting round to get one last look at him.

For a moment the sun blinds her, flashing off her glasses, flashing a Morse return from the flat glass panes of the Rectory windows. She takes her glasses off and squints into the sun across the graveyard, across the grassy paddock beyond the graveyard fence, but there's no sign of him. Just the open gate, the driveway twisting across the empty paddock to the redbrick gateposts of the Rectory. The gates are open there too, a white van parked on the dusty forecourt, its tailgate open. Tall sandy weeds cluster round the doorstep. There's a sound of knocking, echoing across the paddock. A man is hammering a *For Sale* board into the grass beside the gatepost. She rubs her eyes, to check it's not a dream.

I look again. No, not a dream. Real life, but with the texture of a dream, the pulse of it. The story thins in my head until it fades into transparency, until through its glass I can see the forms and shapes of real life. I'm standing in the churchyard, my mother's grave behind me, facing the empty Rectory. Turned on my axis, back towards Wilford.

Time passes. I ease myself into my own skin slowly, not knowing quite how to wear it. Around me the world, as it has so often done, seems an extension of myself, but one now visible in the open air. The world has become full of signs and portents, all turning me back towards the village. Or back towards myself; it's hard to tell, hard to find the moment when this particular narrative slipped between the pages of the novel I am writing. The moment of epiphany in the therapist's room, the tutor's *We'd rather have a story*; Alex, giving me the finger of his continued existence five years after Reed's death, each year planning another comeback. Old neighbours have found me out, left messages on the answerphone in voices I haven't heard in twenty years. On Wednesdays Wilford Church is open for quiet prayer, and I have been inside, reached my mother's embroidered kneelers from beneath the pews, knelt on the blue and yellow crosses shaped by her stitchery. At night I dream of the church again and again, processing down the aisle in my graduation gown, a remembrance poppy on my soft black hat; or of visiting my grandparents, watching the smoke from my Grandpa's Navy Cut drifting behind him like the steam-trail of a locomotive. There are feelings in these dreams, dark patches of silence in sitting-rooms that are stopped in time, questions emanating from the members of my family – why have I stayed away so long? – but nobody is dead, nobody ill.

By 2007 I know that I want to go home to Wilford. It's strange to me to know how I feel, troubling to be so obvious, so stripped down to a primal impulse. My writer's self wants to know if I am driving events, or being driven, but the self that trawls the websites for vacant possession, that tracks cousins in America to cousins slightly less distant, doesn't care. The signs are all, and they come fast and thick with meaning. For several months, we hover over the purchase of a property on Vernon Avenue, a large house with a tiny fruiting plum tree in the back garden. The house is beyond our means, but I can see the dark juice of the fruit on my hands as I climb the tree, juice dark as ink. And I see the view from the second floor, so high that the old boundary of the railway line appears above the rooftops.

And then, in late October, my husband calls to me from his office:

I think your old house is for sale.

I go in and look over his shoulder at the details on the screen. *Wilford Village*, says the agent's blurb, *Vernon Avenue. Impressive 3 bed 1930s semi, completely refurbished. Oh, my God*, I say, not in surprise but as if I have known all along. I examine the neatened frontage and the tell-tale rise of the ground behind the house in the photo, but I don't really need proof. The date is set for viewing, falling into place beside the house sale; November the 12th, the agent says, if you can make it. And before the viewing, we will spend the eleventh hour of the eleventh day in Wilford Church, at the Remembrance Day service. To be quite sure, before taking this final step, that I am reading the signs correctly, that this story will end as I expect.

Oh, that's not the Rectory any more, says the sidesman, handing me an Order of Service. It's the new bungalow next to the church hall now.

Thanks, I say. We smile at each other. I've come to church, I want to say, the church where I was

250

christened and married, where my mother was christened and married, but I don't say it. He doesn't know me, can't remember.

I look up. Above the old sandstone arches, the ultramarine roof with the yellow stars; before me in the East window Jesus standing foursquare in a white robe flushed with pink, his right hand raised; the Wilford Jesus, not the cadaver of crucifixions but a Michelangelesque Christ, sturdy and well-made, with a high untroubled brow. I look for the choir, but there is no choir, not as I remember it. No procession of gowned choristers, but three or four sweet-voiced parishioners singing a mist of a song as the Remembrance procession enters the church: gentle, unrecognizable but unmistakably secular. They don't process, they don't go to the choirstalls.

Time for the congregation to stand and sing. Not a hymn from Ancient and Modern, but three strange verses entitled *Song*. The tune, as expected, is unknown to me: uptempo, cheery, the words stripped of poetry. Only the words of the Act of Remembrance are unchanged.

*We will remember them.*

*Join our church family*, exhorts the flyer enclosed in our Order of Service. But I joined fifty years ago, when I was christened in the font that is barely a yard from where I am sitting.

Pew by pew is emptying as the parishioners go up to the rail to receive communion. In the Order of

Service it says that those who do not normally receive communion may go up too, and, if they do not normally receive communion, should keep their hands by their sides to signify that they will not take the bread and wine, but will receive a prayer instead.

*Do not normally receive.* I read the words, and read again. Christened, but I did not stay to earn the white dress of confirmation, the black robes of a chorister; I never took my place in the carved choirstalls flanking the risen Christ. I shift in my seat. I hear myself singing the song I made up when I was a child: *Oh, wonderful day*, the swing creaking in my hands, my feet scuffing the ground. The young woman who is moving down the pews, gently shepherding people in and out, has reached our pew.

Would you like to go, she says.

I move out from the pew, following the others up the aisle, up the one step into the choir, onto the scarlet carpet. Jesus is close to me now in his window, the morning light fleshing out his pink robe, but I do not even look up. The faithful kneel and lift their faces to receive the Host. The curate comes to me, a woman with a kindly face, a basket of bread in her hand.

I shut my eyes. My imagined gown brushes the carpet beneath my feet, my mortarboard softens into the cloth hat of a chorister. And then I open my eyes and turn round, and the church is full of strangers. I'm standing beside the choirstalls, but they are empty; nobody is singing.

My lips part. Not for communion, but for the chance to speak, to sing. I think of the tutor, *We'd rather have a story*, I think of the woman sitting on the stairs, my mother's scarf bandaging her head. And I hear my voice, doing something terrible; breaking the silence.

Not here, though; not in this church, not in this family. Silent, I receive my prayer, go back to my place. Silent, I am not really here at all.

As the service finishes, the parishioners make their way down the path to the church hall, to set out chairs where the audience for the Wilford Players used to sit, to drink tea and coffee and celebrate their new community. *Join our church family*. Outside, a smell of new timber wafts toward us in the air. I look left, across the graveyard to the old Rectory. There's a new fence around the garden, a band of raw orange wood encircling the stand of ancient trees, a modern bailey defending the ancient estate. High on the building, whistling a formless tune, a builder with hammer and nails casually straddles the apex of the roof. In front of me the parishioners keep their heads lowered, looking neither left nor right. I want to place my hand on someone's shoulder, I want to say to them, on this day of all days: *Remember*. Instead I leave the new church family, and turn right towards the graveyard, my poppy still in my hand.

Back home, I put the Order of Service away, and take out the agent's details once again. It's then I remember that the God of my childhood was not inside the church at all.

The garden gate – which used to be a simple one of wooden slats that I could crouch behind and peer out at the world – has broadened to the width of a field-gate. I open it and go up to the front door. Number 30 being the end of the terraced row, its front door is on the side of the house, the garden a three-sided plot of land wrapped around the building. In 1955 the trains were a ballast-throw away from the doorstep; fifty years later, a garage casts a brown shadow on the front door; a green cumulus of trees darkens the railway bank above the garage roof.

Home at last, I say to my husband, and while we wait for the vendor he wanders and peers and asks me questions about how the house used to be. I am ready for this; I have done my research. Of all my stories, I must be able to claim this one, I must go to this viewing knowing it by heart. I have been up half the night with old photo albums, looking for the truth of how it was; going through old black and white photos glued tight to porous paper; tiny photos, precious as penny blacks. At first, just my parents, laying claim to their first home together. A photo of my father, smiling, shirtsleeves rolled up, digging in a dark triangle of earth at the bottom of the garden, with the simple fence and the ballast slope behind him; of my mother, sitting in the open doorway on a bright day, her loose printed skirt hitched above her knees, her arms hanging loose at her sides. Then photos of me, first in winter, headscarfed and coated, peeping round the corner of the house with washing flapping in the breeze; to my right the fence again and the clean slope of the railway bank rising up behind it. Next, in summer, making sand-pies in a pit just below the doorstep, my head on one side, as if I am trying to see inside the camera's eye. Smiling, like my parents, in a world small enough to see its boundaries: each edge of it, each surface known by heart.

But there is something about the summer photo that blurs this clarity. The picture itself is more blurred than the winter scene, the tones losing contrast in the flat light of summer, or the photographer stumbling, perhaps, as the shutter clicks. But something else is not quite right, as if the photograph has been tampered with. I can't work out what part of the image is at fault: the soft drapery of the rockery plants below me, the three sandpies ranged in front of me, the smooth brick of the house wall rising above my tilted head. I look into the

255

eyes of my own enquiring face, at the child peering into the recessed pebble of the lens; I stare back at her with the same intensity, the same unrestful need to discover who is behind the camera, whose cropped view of the world she is inhabiting. I worry the problem into the night, scanning each pale grey oblong of brick in the summer photo, not quite knowing why, until I drift into a muddled sleep. And I dream of sleep: curled up on the doorstep, the dark shell of the porch around me.

Aren't you going to knock? says my husband.

We stand back and wait. I didn't ask the vendor's name, I don't even know if he or she is inside. I peer through the hard curls of the baffle glass and imagine my mother coming to the door, hands white with flour, the whistle of the kettle sounding through the house. I want her to be here so that I can reverse the moment in 1961 when I left the house where I was born, Panda with his browless eyes swinging from my hand; the moment when someone else took possession. I imagine going up the stairs behind her to the room with the pink nightlight, where *The Wind in the Willows* lies on the cupboard beside my bed, open at *Dulce Domum*, the chapter which always made me cry. And I think of the house receiving me back, like Mole's neglected burrow, without rancour, of the story bending back upon itself until the ending touches the beginning. With the lightest touch; as light as my mother's.

But when I have knocked for the second time, and nobody has answered, I already know that the house is empty.

A car pulls up outside the house. A middle-aged couple – strangers - get out.

Sorry we're a bit late, says the man.

He unlocks the door. We are ushered into the hall, the stairs off to our right, the front room to our left. No furniture, just a damp skin of new plaster on the walls and the sweet smell of timber rising from the floors. New floors, new windows, new treads to the stairs – bespoke kitchen, says the vendor, to the rear.

We follow him through to the back of the house. Fitted kitchen cupboards run along the rear house wall, with a Belfast sink beneath the window that looks out over the back garden. The vendor crouches to display joints and finishes. I look along the length of the wall: at the window, at the sink beneath it, at the back door close to the house corner. The feeling of incongruence returns, but now I know what is wrong, what has been tampered with. The inside of the house is twisted round from its orientation in my memory. I see my mother at the sink, soap suds braceleting her wrists, looking out of the window – but the kitchen window should face the side of the house, not the rear. The kitchen is in the wrong place; it should be where the stairs are now. I go back out into the hallway, interrogate the vendor, but he is adamant that the stairs are where they always were.

I remember it differently, I say, and he looks at me. Before he can ask why, I have disappeared through the back door into the garden: down the concrete steps onto the small square lawn, turning to face the house so that the rockery is in front of me, the railway bank behind. The kitchen window peers right back at me, not where it should be; yet where it is, stubborn, fixed. There is one way only to move it.

I run the memory. I am four years old, and there is a swan in the garden. I skip up the rockery steps to the back door to amaze my mother with the news. At the sink my mother is washing my father's shirt, the green brick of Fairy on the board beside her. I tell her about the swan, but she does not come to look. Because the kitchen window does not face the garden, my mother cannot see the swan; she has only my word for its existence. She smiles at me and nods; the swan is one of my stories, charming, but only a white bird in my head. I go outside again. The white bird has a voice: the hiss of gas before the match is struck, before the burst of fire. She has tried to take off, and failed; folded her wings in despair. Inside the kitchen, the washing piles on the draining board, glittering in its suds. Only when it is finished, ready to be pegged out on the line, does my mother come outside, and see the swan.

And, Oh, she says; There really is a swan.

I am vindicated; yet somehow left with the ghost of an unreal swan, the story that was not believed. The real swan is taken away, her story incomplete. I don't know if she had a happy ending. Two swans, two stories, all my life.

But it turns out that the memory is one of my stories after all. There is no kitchen window in the side wall of the house: no window in the side wall shown in the photograph, none here, looking from the green-rug garden, fifty years later. The kitchen window looks over the garden. My mother must have seen the swan, but did not come outside. Or did she? It's possible to stand at the window and look, not down into the garden, but out to the railway bank, to watch for the long dark trace of the next train; it's possible to see, not what is in front of the eyes, but something held back behind them, a picture in the mind. Perhaps her surprise was feigned; one of her roles, assumed before I had ever seen her act.

*Perhaps.* The stories multiply in my head. The past unravels.

So you knew the house before, then, the vendor says as I go back inside.

A long time ago, I say.

A pause. They look at me.

I was born here, I say. I'm Sheila's daughter. Sheila Plumb.

They shake their heads.

That's before our time, I think, says the vendor.

We still have the upstairs to view. My husband heads for the front bedroom, but it's the back bedroom – my bedroom - I want to see. Stripped back of any history, like the downstairs: sandy walls the colour of the brick outside, windows open to let out the sweat of the plaster. I go to the window and look out. The trees have their bones well into the bank, their canopies eat up the sky. I feel for the memory of a train, for the image of the waving guard, but it won't come. Number 30 stands how it is, foursquare in my way, pulling away the scraps of truth I thought I held.

And then I think I smell a train. There are dark spots of soot outside, drifting in the air. Not just soot but embers and thin black ashes, some disintegrating as they hit the air, some of them blown by the easterly through the open window, circling like flies in the room before settling on the floorboards. Black-bordered flakes of newspaper, with scraps of words in their centres that the flame hasn't reached. I look outside for the fire, scanning the trees, the small square lawn below me. A wisp of smoke slips over the ragged hedge. In the centre of the garden next door is an old metal dustbin, a plume of smoke rising from its makeshift chimney. Lidless, streaked with soot and filled with half-burned rubbish: clothes, old newspapers, it's hard to tell. Smoking, gently, unattended. There's nobody there.

My husband glances at me as I get back into the car.

You look as if you've seen a ghost, he says.

I shake my head and look out of the window.

I don't think you want to move back after all, he says.

But I do go back, that night, when the vendor has locked up and gone home. I dream myself across the old Toll Bridge, the river dark as ink beneath me, I dream myself down the lamplit avenue and into the house, into my bedroom with the pink nightlight softening the edges of the room, up to the window, looking out of the window for the goods train and the guard with the black peaked cap. It's dark and I can't see him. Below me I can see that the back door is open and a wedge of light let into the garden. My mother stands in its spotlight, headscarfed, coated, standing over the smoking bin, burning papers. The words on them melting into the smoke.

I bang on the window, call out for her to stop. She turns at the sound and looks upward, but her gaze is too high, beyond the window and the house roof.

As she turns, I realize she doesn't have her glasses on. She can't see me.


A second time, I emerge from the dream. I am in the spare room, the box of my mother's things open beside me.

# *19*

# *Bridge*

The agent phones, wanting to know if we are still interested in the house. Oh, yes, I say, but we're thinking about it. Well, don't think too long, she says, and I assent and put down the phone. I am thinking, but not quite in the way she imagines. I have retraced my life, gone back as far as I can go and forward again; and still I can't complete this story. My mother's story is still running in my mind, and I know that it must be finished before my own can be laid to rest. That I *can* finish it, from the trail of enigmatic clues she left behind her, is a new thought, accompanied by a strange, shaky feeling akin to the old panic, the knowledge that I am about to find something she would have kept from me; a nervous wish for reassurance where there can be none. A thin voice in my head – I must do this – squeaks insect-sharp as Al Hedison's voice in *The Fly*. But insistent, audible – just. I shut the door and begin to take my mother's things from the green metal box on the floor in front of me.

I am still wrestling with the meaning of the dream. Sometimes I imagine my mother has burnt her story, sometimes it seems to me – as in life – that she has left sufficient clues for me to find it out. Her possessions are laid carefully out on the carpet: the pilot's scarf, the newspaper cutting of Douglas Bader's visitation; Elvira's costume, grey as a shroud, from which Charles flees across the water; more things in Heaven and Earth.

There is the Drama Scrapbook, her walnut jewellery box with the broken lock, her paintings. I have the play-texts where her roles are underlined; unused notebooks whose blank pages are crammed with her silences. No surprises, nothing I haven't seen before. But, as at number 30, there has to be something I have missed. I can recall her commonplace book, a hardbound notebook whose marbled covers have been sleeved in brown paper; but taking it out this time I notice that there are faint, handwritten words on the paper, words I can't quite make out. Inside the book, my mother's youthful writing begins neat and anonymous, slowly reshaping itself into the familiar, windblown letters of her mature hand as she copies the words of Romantic and pastoral poets, Hardy, Housman, Browning, Shakespeare: words between the words, wherever I look, but always the words of other writers between us. *All the world's a stage; If I should die, think only this of me.* None of the entries is dated, but most of them are written in blue fountain pen; the last couple in black biro.

Predictably, perhaps, few women, but last of all a woman: Stevie Smith, and her poem of a dead man speaking: *Not Waving but Drowning*. Beneath the poem, my mother has added a footnote, in brackets, but her own words: *For he, read <u>she</u>.*

I know the poem well enough, but I read it again. Plain, bleak, the words too dark, too shaky for my mother's steady hand, more suited to my own tremulous writing. This is how it was, at the end of her life: a woman whose distress was silent and unheard; unheard, because silent. But silence was not a quality that came late to her; it stretches back and back in my memory, as dateless as the entry in the book. My quiet, secretive mother; not just becoming so as family and village life crumbles but so at the beginning, or, at any rate, the only beginning I can retrieve.

A second time, I take myself as far back as I can go: back to number 30, climbing on the fence to wave at the guard as a goods train passes. I place my mother where I now know she was: looking out, over the garden, from behind the glass of the kitchen window. At my back, beyond my field of vision, she too is waving, her hand glistening with suds, veins of water running down her arm. The guard returns my wave and tips his glossy cap. Out of the sky the white bird with her spread wings and great black feet comes down to land in my garden, and I turn from the guard and watch her approach with wonder. But my mother, hand still raised, is watching the departing train; rolling towards its vanishing point.

I look back at the book again. The pages that follow the poem - perhaps twenty of them - are blank to the end of the book. Slipped in behind the last page is a folded sheet of cartridge paper. Inside it is one of my teenage drawings for a painting, entitled *Strain*: a nude, androgynous figure, head thrown back, outstretched arms braced against encroaching walls. I remove the drawing, exposing the back board of the book with its brown paper cover. Behind the drawing, a pressed sprig of maroon heather crumbles into the spine, and a pocket calendar for 1943 sits like a photograph in the frame of the paper sleeve. Beneath the calendar, there is a loose sheet of paper tucked into a fold of the brown cover.

Another poem. But this one is not written in my mother's hand. It is addressed to her, in a loose, looping script: *To Sheila*. I pick it up and read the first two stanzas:

> *I went into the library*
> *One dull, dark winter's day*
> *I went to get a book to read,*
> *To chase the gloom away.*
>
> *I didn't have to look for books,*
> *For just beyond the door,*
> *I saw you Sheila dearest,*
> *I wanted nothing more.*

I know who wrote this poem. I know it was my mother's fiancé, the airman, the owner of the scarf. I know that this is the last piece of evidence for my mother's former life, the end of the trail of clues; the plays, the Bader cutting, the scarf, all leading up to this discovery. But the rest is history, irretrievable: my mother is not in front of me, talking, stitching her possessions together into a whole. The objects are spread out on the floor around me: the jewellery box, the envelope with the cutting, the scarf, the calendar; the poem; connected but separate. Kim's game, I think. Take them away and I might not remember them.

The commonplace book is still in my hand. I flick the blank pages, once, and again. They tempt me. A thought occurs: The truth is not so very different from fiction after all. At some point, we must go beyond what we can know. And, perhaps, I know more than I think I do. I do not look just outside my self at the objects, but inside too, into my head where my own life is stored, written back into my consciousness: Wilford, the Toll Bridge, Southern. I see myself, at the Meadows Library in 1986, stamping books, looking toward the open oak doors; I see the inner door open, and a young man come in, asking for my colleague. I remember the young man's name.

So I go beyond what I know. Push the time back slowly, until images and invention fuse in the mind, until it is my mother, not myself, at the issue desk, in 1943; the door opening to reveal the airman, in uniform, the silk scarf around his neck. I suspend, not disbelief, but self. Pick up the pen and put myself aside, the way I've always done.


He comes on the heels of the all-clear, the siren winding down its wail across the Meadows, bringing out the shoppers and the borrowers into the streets, filling the library with soldiers whose greatcoats are musty with rain and smoke; soldiers who bite their cigarettes, hush quickly into quiet and bend their heads over newspapers and books in the Reading Room. The word SILENCE, on a wooden board, suspended from the ceiling. No loose talk here, costing lives: the library has the cool quiet air of a church amid the chaos of the war. Lights on, burning like the sacred flame; the tall sash windows chequered squares of blackout.

The library door opens, then swings shut again. Sheila Bailey looks up briefly and bends her head again to the pile of books before her on the fumed oak issue desk. The young man sits scribbling at a table. His uniform the slate-blue of the RAF, white arched wings over the cigarettes in his breast pocket. He has an Ivor Novello face, grown up too soon. The girl at the counter has it too: eighteen, with four years of war, each year a decade of maturity, behind her. They speak briefly together, exchange their names; they each confess a love of poetry. The airman watches her as he reads, as he writes his poem *To Sheila*; a simple poem, but graceful. As he writes, he can form words that do not stumble, tell her his feelings without being overheard. Finished, he tucks the poem in his library book and takes it to the desk, for her to stamp. She opens it and sees the paper in his hand. When he is gone she reads it.

What's his name, then, says her colleague, leaning over her shoulder.

John, she says. John.

At eight o'clock the library girls pull the oak doors to and lock them. Outside, the torch of Ted's Navy Cut glows red as he waits on the nib of the junction to walk his daughter home. Through the dull Meadows streets with their blank windows, along the loop of the Embankment, across the Toll Bridge. The river is lit gunmetal grey from somewhere: a half-moon, starlight, a searchlight stretched thin across the sky, picking up the shine on the surface of the water, the mounds of swirling current banked up as if over the bodies of strangers who have fallen through on moonless nights. Bursts of white light in the sky; the Power Station chimneys stand out black, then fade to dark again. Sheila's right arm firmly hooked into her father's arm, her left hand curled around the poem in her pocket.

You're preoccupied tonight, her father says.

In weeks John and Sheila are engaged. She has his picture in a heart-shaped locket on her charm bracelet, his serious face looking across the hinge to the space where she will set a photograph of herself. He is called away on Operations, but the war is turning; they will be married soon. Sheila stamps books and watches the borrowers in and out between the sandstone columns of the library, Meadows boys and boys from anywhere in airforce blue and khaki; she feels the skip in her chest when the uniform is blue. She hears no news; not soon, not later. When her father brings the official letter to her at work, she takes the brown envelope quietly in her hand and goes to the back of the library to open it. Her back turned to the borrowers, the sign requesting Silence over her head.

It takes longer for the scarf to be sent to her. Somehow she imagines John flying over the map drawn out on the silk, the names of the places she has never been stark against the expanse of dark bruised land. For months afterwards the words, all words, hurt her eyes: she can only bear them behind the blackout of dark glasses. She hides in the cinema, watching the pictures carried to the screen in the smoky wedge of light. Not only Noël Coward's clipped heroics but another film –

*The Way to the Stars* - about the sacrifice of war. One woman's sacrifice touches her most closely: the widow of a pilot who has been shot down. But the pilot has left her something: a poem. More than a poem. A way to live her life without him.

The pilot's widow cannot read the poem when it is brought to her; she does not have her glasses. Instead she asks her husband's comrade to read it. The words of the poem: *air, clouds, stars*, soar upward; the reading is clumsy and awkward, bringing the words down like birds to the ground. The widow listens, her face blank, setting into stillness. Later, she will offer the wisdom of the poem to others: freely, for comfort, passing it on as if she cannot bear its weight alone.

Sheila does not write this poem into her book. She keeps its words unspoken in her mind, its title - *For Johnny* - committed to memory, like the phantom image of her photograph in the locket. The film ends, the war ends. The safety curtain of the blackout lifts on a world of austerity and iron winters. In 1947, icicles hang from the arches of the railway viaduct; the Trent hoards ice until the thaw, letting out its flood into the village, drowning fields and roads, marooning the Toll Bridge in a tideless sea. Every house is an island, its supplies tractored in along the shallow stream of the main road. Sheila and her parents live upstairs, looking out over the melted land. At the foot of the stairs, through the dirty water, a glimpse of mud, like the trenches in her father's memory.

Finally the sun shines. The river falls back on its curve, leaving its wreckage on the land like the aftermath of an incendiary. Sheila and her cousin, also bereaved of a fiancé in the war, take a holiday together in the Lakes. At another cousin's wedding she meets Robert, fresh from Palestine. There is warmth and affection between them; no poetry but prose, good sense, a future. Sheila writes a letter, announcing her forthcoming marriage; the Library authorities thank her for her service. On her last day at Southern she extinguishes the lights, and piece by piece her library disappears: the cupola, the bookstacks, the sign requesting Silence; the table where John sat to write his poem. For a moment, the blackout returns.

There is a national housing shortage, but Robert and Sheila have the good fortune to find a modest house for rent in Wilford soon after their marriage. Sheila busies herself making a home, but the loss of her library aches through the stillness of her day. A self she thinks she has put away listens to the night trains, counts the rhythms of poetry without the words. In 1951, three years after her marriage, she begins the Drama Group. The Wilford Players will not perform the hard drama of the new age, full of disharmony and complaint, but Noël Coward's plays, scripted straight from Johnny's wartime world, words bandaged around the words that are too raw to show. On Thursday nights Sheila dresses in the lives of women like the pilot's widow, women worthy of Johnny: Laura, Ethel, Elvira. A ghost of her former self, spotlit in Elvira's grey draperies, a shroud by any other name: dead, yet light as air, not grieving.

There are real bandages now, in Sheila's second life, as she bends over her daughter's split knee. *Hush,* she says, while her daughter wails, putting her gentle hand over the red burn of the graze, winding the blood away under the white of the bandage; *hush*, as they walk together to the clinic where her daughter must be left alone; as she walks home with her own story pinned tight behind her lips. Never telling; believing silence is best; maintaining it almost to the last.

Perhaps Sheila forgets, sometimes, that this is not John's daughter. But the daughter of her second life, who never hushes, who always scents the truth behind her mother's small kindly lies; who screams her way through panic, through the riverbank assault, who will not take silence for an answer. But she will remember at the end, in hospital, her paper rested on a white sheet as she writes a last note to her daughter, seals the envelope and the words inside it: *Forgive me for my mistakes.*

I take the pen from the page, leave a blank line. Then I add one more sentence:

*Forgive me for telling.*


My hand is shaking. I uncurl my fingers from the pen and flex them. Then I close the book, and place it gently on the carpet. I shut my eyes, and it is there; open them again, and it is still there. I look at it a long time, building it into my memory, until my hands cool and the chill of the room begins to travel up my limbs. Beside me the green box is still open. Underneath the place where the book was lying there is a brown envelope, addressed to my father at 30 Vernon Avenue. Inside the envelope, a sheaf of childish drawings secured by a rusted paperclip. And a typed note from a national newspaper, dated 1958, commenting kindly on the potential of the four-year-old artist.

As I ease the paperclip away it leaves a mark, a rusty, iron-red loop on the topmost paper. My childhood drawings fall into my lap: a loose-leaf record of my early life in pictures, a record made before fear and silence and words took hold. And I have drawn my whole four-year old world, Wilford as it was to me then: the village; the furniture in my house; stick children on the swings in the Embankment playground; Red Indians with startled headdresses; the characters in Alice in Wonderland. Several times Wilford Church appears, its roof zigzagged with dragon-back castellations, a fat S of a weathervane atop its spiky tower; over and over again the procession of the choir into church, a centipede of long flowing gowns and small heads under the squares of soft felt hats. A world of pictures which seems clear enough to me, but to which my father has added words: additional sheets of annotations, explaining for the benefit of the *News Chronicle* what each object represents.

In at least one case he is wrong. I have drawn my bedroom at number 30, every piece of furniture carefully represented: chairs, wardrobes, chest of drawers and nightlight, narrow skirted single bed. A tall figure, in chorister's robes and hat, stands over the bed. My father has labelled this figure 'a choir lady,' but I recognize my mother's curls bubbling from the hat, the thin frames of her spectacles, the pencil blur of her mouth. At the head of the bed are a teddy bear and a doll; a flat dark pillow in front of them. Further down, in the middle of the bedspread, a doorstep of a book – 'Alice' perhaps – with a girl's smiling face on the cover.

It is my bed, clearly enough: bedtime, or time to get up, presumably, with my mother standing over me to rouse me, or read me into sleep. But I am not there.

I go through the drawings again, looking for myself. I make only one appearance, and I have added my name in capitals so that there can be no confusion. I am in a garden – there are trees either side of me – but the flowers are on my dress, a fifties flared number with a full skirt. I am smiling, holding a basket; the pointed hat of a chorister, or a graduand, is on my head. My feet are skipping, but they can't go far, because I am inside a fenced enclosure. Outside the enclosure, a more muddled scribble, but recognizably the figure of the Red Queen from Alice: the executioner. She leans over the fence, but she can't cross it. My smile is fixed, my head turned away from her, but I know she is there. My father's annotation calls her the 'Cross Queen,' but the girl in the flowered dress is labelled 'Alice,' ignoring the capitals of my name above the figure. He is wrong again, or is he? This is not a picture of Roberta's real life in the external world, a child climbing the garden fence to wave to God. Already, in this drawing, I am disappearing into a second life of character, fencing out the terrors of the external world in a stockade of pencil-strokes. A gentle world, a stranger would think, a world of choirs and gardens and loving parents; no terrors, no Red Queen obvious anywhere. But the smiling girl in the

273

flowery dress knows that Wonderland is bordered by the fence, and she has a child's instinct for what lies in the silence beyond it: loss and sorrow, the grown-up words her mother will not speak.

I park the car and start to walk slowly up the slope towards the Toll Bridge. Today I'm thinking of endings, real and unreal; trying to choose one that belongs, that sounds a real note in my head. I think of my Sebastian, whom I left on the bank of another river, facing across the unbridged water to his mother on the other side; I think of Alex, his death in the real world still raw and recent, shrinking back inside his clothes until he seemed almost to dissolve on the air. And I think of the ending I thought was being written for me, going home to a house that had remained, like Mole's, as I remembered it; with parents who – in the way of childhood stories - were waiting for me, benign ghosts always with me at the table when I sat down to write. I know now that this is a yearning, one that will never leave me; but not the place where this story ends.

Number 30 is sold. I don't know who the buyer is; I haven't asked. My Wilford has receded once again, but not back into a lost history, not back into the box of my mother's things. Words anchor my history to the ground now, a story that will let me go back and back at will; like dreams, but more solid. And I am closer to home in my dreams than inside its walls; like Mole, I recognize that we cannot go back, but must.

It's windy today, a wind driving from the south and pushing against the north bank of the river, like the tongue of the Wilford isthmus; windy enough to make me stop on top of the bridge and shelter in the foliage of a tree and look down at the river beneath me. The riverside willows have grown into great tall trees, one of them so high an arm of branches reaches over the handrail of the bridge, curving and growing over the span as if trying to arch right across to the other side. The wind blows its leaves against my face. I look right, toward the village, but I don't move. I let my hands wrap around the balustrade, let the green rail support my body. I feel almost at ease here, almost still, almost solid, despite the stirred inky water beneath me. The bridge does not change the fact of the river; we are all sundered from each other, from our histories, from ourselves. But it holds on, this patched structure of new green steel and old brick turrets.

As I lean there I see people coming towards me from the Wilford side, a dark mass of schoolchildren taking a diagonal track across the unfenced Ferry field on their way towards the bridge. They begin to file past me, laughing, their bike wheels swishing on the tarmac. There's still a school on the site where I feared I would go if I failed the 11 plus, but the old black uniforms of the Deering have softened into Clifton purple; their school is renamed the Wilford Emmanuel School. On the far side of the railway bank, the place I couldn't see from my garden, God passed by them as well. They don't shout challenges or leap on me, just leave a change in the air as they pass, a tear in the fabric of the real; so that briefly, when I look round at them, I see someone else - a studious girl with a look of my mother, a faint grey child waiting for a name. When I turn back to the river there are spots on the water in the distance, pale spots that might be swans or geese. I press down on the green rail and stand my ground. The flow of children eases and it's quiet again.

There's the sound of a disturbance in the water behind me. Like the slap of oars. I look down and from underneath the bridge she appears, first her head, beak inked and slim, then her long white neck. Her wings scull the water, her great black feet tread water as she gathers speed. Then she tucks her feet behind her, trusts her weight to the wings and she's held above the water, a golden space beneath her, the space between her body and the river, that never varies. As she flies away she's straight as a die, only adjusting her course to curve around the pier of the railway bridge that only she and I can see, turning gracefully with the bend of the river. I hear the rhythm of her wings, like the beat of a sail in a high wind. Echoing, deepening, as she flies.

## *Acknowledgements*

This book has been long in the making, and many people have helped me along the way, but those who have been with this narrative longest are the members of my workshop group, who have patiently seen it through childhood, adolescence, and into maturity, and offered wisdom and encouragement at each stage: Diana, Vicky, and Joy. Thanks must also go to Rod Duncan, who read the full manuscript for me, and whose wonderful insights helped me to see the book as a whole for the first time; and to all those in the writing community in Nottingham who offered sage advice, including Ross Bradshaw of Five Leaves, who published a part of *The Power House* in *Maps* (2011). On a more personal level, thanks to those friends who agreed to appear in this story, and especially to my husband Peter who has been with the project from the outset, helping with travel, technology, and all those things with which I struggle. And, of course, my family, most of whom I couldn't ask if they were happy to appear, but who I have tried to show with the kindness and sympathy they deserve. This has been a journey into understanding. Thanks to everyone who accompanied me.

*The Memory of Bridges*